# GLOBETROTTER™

## Travel Guide

# PHILIPPINES

## NIGEL HICKS

NEW
HOLLAND

NEW
HOLLAND

★★★ Highly recommended
★★ Recommended
★ See if you can

Fifth edition published in 2010
by New Holland Publishers (UK) Ltd
London • Cape Town • Sydney • Auckland
10 9 8 7 6 5 4 3 2 1

website: www.newhollandpublishers.com

Garfield House, 86 Edgware Road,
London W2 2EA United Kingdom

80 McKenzie Street
Cape Town 8001 South Africa

Unit 1, 66 Gibbes Street
Chatswood NSW 2067 Australia

218 Lake Road
Northcote, Auckland New Zealand

Distributed in the USA by The Globe Pequot Press
Connecticut

ISBN 978 1 84773 835 6

**Keep us Current:**
Information in travel guides is apt to change, which is
why we regularly update our guides. We'd be grateful to
receive feedback if you've noted something we should
include in our updates. If you have new information,
please share it with us by writing to the Publishing
Manager, Globetrotter, at the office nearest to you
(addresses on this page). The most significant contribution
to each new edition will receive a free copy of the
updated guide.

**Publishing Manager:** Thea Grobbelaar
**DTP Cartographic Manager:** Genené Hart
**Cartographers:** Reneé Spocter, Rudi de Lange,
Genené Hart
**Editors:** Thea Grobbelaar, Carla Redelinghuys,
Melany Porter, Mary Duncan, Peter Duncan
**Design and DTP:** Nicole Bannister, Eloïse Moss
**Picture researchers:** Shavonne Govender, Rowena Curtis
Reproduction by Hirt & Carter (Pty) Ltd, Cape Town.
Printed and bound by Times Offset (M) Sdn. Bhd., Malaysia.

**Photographic credits:**
**Travel Pix Collection/awl-images.com:** cover; **Mary Evans
Picture Library:** pages 13, 17; **Nigel Hicks:** pages 6, 7, 9, 10,
11, 16, 19, 20, 22, 24, 25, 28, 29, 30, 33, 35, 36, 37, 38,
44, 45, 46, 47, 48, 49, 50, 51, 52, 53, 55, 58, 60, 61, 62,
63, 64, 65, 66, 67, 70, 72, 73, 74, 75, 76, 77, 78, 79, 82,
84, 86, 87, 88, 89, 90, 91, 92 (top and bottom), 93, 96, 98,
99, 100, 101, 102, 103, 108, 110, 111, 112, 113, 114, 115,
116, 117, 118, 119 (top and bottom); **Norma Joseph:** title
page, pages 4, 8, 12, 15, 18, 21, 26 (top and bottom), 39,
42, 54; **Photo Access:** page 104.

**Cover:** *Jeepneys in the Makati Financial District, Manila.*
**Title page:** *White Beach, Boracay Island.*

# CONTENTS

# 1
# Introducing the Philippines

The Philippines is a sprawling tropical archipelago of over 7000 islands, stretching from close to Borneo in the southwest almost as far as Taiwan in the north. Most of the larger islands are mountainous with numerous volcanoes, a reflection of the country's location on the **Pacific Ring of Fire**. Many of the smaller islands are the tops of coral reefs, and some are low-lying, ringed by the spectacular white beaches for which the country has become famous. Beneath the waves are extensive coral reefs that both protect the shore from storms and provide a home to a wealth of marine life.

It is this natural beauty that draws people to the Philippines. The principal attraction is the tiny island of **Boracay**, with its stunning white beaches and azure sea, but there are other beach resorts that draw their share of visitors, such as **Puerto Galera**, **El Nido**, and **Panglao Island**. The country is also becoming one the world's great **diving** centres, with some magnificent reefs now accessible, especially those close to the beach resorts.

Inland, many visitors head up into the mountains of northern Luzon, known as the **Cordillera Central**, particularly to the city of **Baguio** and the rice terraces around **Banaue**.

Historical interest hinges mostly around the remains of Spain's 350-year colonial rule. There are several beautiful **churches** from this period, and in addition there is **Intramuros**, the old walled section of the capital city, Manila, and **Vigan**, an almost intact Spanish town that was once the capital of the far north.

## Top Attractions

*** **Boracay:** spectacular beaches and resort facilities.
*** **Alona Beach:** good facilities, excellent diving.
*** **El Nido:** sheer cliffs and isolated beaches.
*** **Sagada:** mountain village surrounded by pine forest, with caves and scenic landscapes.
** **Puerto Galera:** several beaches, world-class diving.
** **Camiguin:** beautiful scenery, an active volcano, hot and cold springs, and extremely friendly people.
** **Banaue:** spectacular mountain-side rice terraces.

**Opposite:** *Ancient rice terraces in the Cordillera Central mountains.*

**Above:** *Sabang beach in Palawan is just one of the Philippines' great beaches.*

## THE LAND

The Philippines is situated on the eastern edge of Asia. It is bounded to the west by the South China Sea and to the east by the Pacific Ocean. Its nearest neighbours are the Malaysian province of Sabah and the Indonesian territory of Kalimantan, both on Borneo to the southwest. Across the South China Sea, about 1000km (620 miles) west, lies Vietnam, and a similar distance to the east are the Palau Islands. China lies about 500km (310 miles) to the north.

### The Islands

Officially, the Philippines consists of 7107 islands, with a land area of almost 300,000km² (116,000 sq miles). There are six major island groups. The largest and most densely populated is **Luzon**, which forms the bulk of the northern landmass and is the site of the capital, Manila. **Mindanao** is the second-largest island, forming the southern landmass. Between is a cluster of islands collectively called the **Visayas**, principal of which are **Panay**, **Negros**, **Cebu**, **Bohol**, **Samar**, **Leyte** and **Masbate**. The fourth region is **Mindoro**, a mountainous island in the southern underbelly of Luzon. Southwestwards towards Borneo is **Palawan**, a long, thin, pencil-like island. Finally, in the far south, are the **Sulu Islands**, running from the western tip of Mindanao to within just a few kilometres of Borneo.

## Coasts and Seas

With such a large number of separate islands, the Philippines has an incredibly long coastline, totalling 36,289km (21,773 miles). The highly indented coast has created 60 natural harbours and there are about 34,000km$^2$ (13,128 sq miles) of **coral reefs**. Beyond the reefs, the seabed around most of the islands plunges away to great depths even within the closely confined waters of the Visayas. Off the Pacific coast the seabed drops into the Philippine Trench, which just east of Mindanao reaches a depth of about 10,500m (34,450ft).

## Mountains and Volcanoes

The Philippine islands are the tips of submerged mountains driven up from the seabed by the impact of the Eurasian and Philippine **tectonic plates** grinding against one another. Most of the resulting mountain chains are orientated north–south, and are subject to **earthquakes**. One of the most devastating in recent times occurred in 1990, seriously damaging the cities of Baguio, Dagupan and Cabanatuan, resulting in 1600 deaths.

The Philippines has over 200 **volcanoes**, 22 of them active. The country's highest peak, **Mount Apo**, is an inactive volcano. The country's most active volcano is **Mount Mayon**, known to have erupted 48 times. Towering over the city of Legaspi, it is famous for its almost perfect cone. South of Manila is a cluster of volcanoes, two of them active. The most dangerous of these – despite being one of the world's smallest volcanoes – is **Taal**. It sits on a small island in the midst of a lake that is said to be itself the caldera of a once huge volcano.

**Below:** *Mount Mayon is renowned for its perfectly conical shape, permanently smouldering crater and frequent eruptions.*

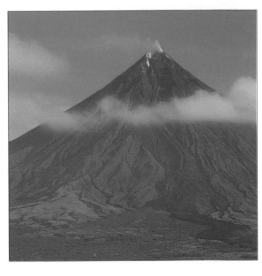

## CLIMATIC VARIATION

Weather patterns, divided mainly into wet and dry, are complicated by relative exposures to the southwest (from June to October) and northeast (from November to May) monsoons. Generally, areas exposed to the former are wet from June to October, and those to the latter are wet from November or December to January or February. Some areas will be wet at both times, though usually only to a moderate degree. All areas are at their driest in April and May, but these are also the hottest months.

**Below:** *A footpath balances atop a tiny dyke in a rice field.*

**Climatic Zones**

Long dry season Nov-May
Intense rain Jun-Oct

Short dry season Mar-May
Moderate rain Jun-Feb

Rain falling during most of the year
Period of maximum rainfall Nov-Feb

No clearly defined dry season
Period of maximum rainfall Apr-Sep

No pronounced wet or dry seasons

PACIFIC OCEAN

Luzon

SOUTH CHINA SEA

Mindoro    Samar

Panay   Cebu

Palawan    Leyte

N

Negros   Bohol

0    200 km

0    100 miles

Mindanao

The most notorious of Philippine volcanoes is **Mount Pinatubo**, situated in the Zambales Mountains, north of Manila. After lying inactive for 450 years, in June 1991 it produced one of the world's largest eruptions of the 20th century, devastating Central Luzon and killing hundreds of people.

## Climate

The Philippines is a tropical country, whose weather is determined by the **southwest** and **northeast monsoons**. The former, blowing from June to October or November, brings heavy rain, while the latter, from November or December to May, tends to be drier, bringing rain mainly to just the exposed east coasts. The country is divided into five **climatic zones**, more or less reflecting relative exposure to these monsoons. Thus, much of the west, including Manila, is very wet from June to November and dry for the rest of the year. Areas open to the northeast monsoon will be wet from December to March. Only in April and May is dry weather certain across the whole country, but these are also the hottest months.

Severe storms known as **typhoons** sweep across the northern half of the country from May to December (usually about 20 per year), travelling in a westerly or northwesterly direction, wreaking havoc on the eastern coasts and causing floods in Manila. Such storms do not affect the southern half of the country.

## Plant and Animal Life

The Philippines has one of the world's highest **biodiversities**, with an extraordinary range of plant and animal species, many **endemic**, or unique, to the country. Thus, 43 per cent of the country's birds and two-thirds of its mammals and higher plants live nowhere else. The reason for this enormous diversity lies mainly in the country's long-held isolation. With the exception of Palawan, the Philippines has not been attached to the Asian landmass in recent geological times. Thus, while Palawan received an influx of animals and plants from Borneo, those in most of the country evolved in isolation, producing quite unique forms.

### UNIQUE WILDLIFE

The Philippines' isolation has ensured that a wealth of unique wildlife has developed. Hunting and loss of habitat have ensured that almost all are endangered. Some of the best known are as follows:
*Mammals*
**Tamaraw:** a form of wild cattle.
**Philippine tarsier:** one of the world's smallest primates.
**Cloud rat:** a large rodent; several species exist.
**Golden-crowned flying fox:** the world's largest fruit bat.
**Bearded and warty pigs:** several species exist in different parts of the country.
**Philippine spotted deer:** survives only in the Visayas.
*Birds*
**Philippine eagle:** the world's second-largest raptor.
**Tarictic hornbill:** several species exist in different parts of the Philippines.
**Palawan hornbill:** lives only in Palawan.
**Philippine cockatoo:** lives in several remote areas of the country.
**Palawan peacock pheasant:** lives only in Palawan.
*Other*
**Philippine or Freshwater crocodile:** survives in several parts of the country.

**Above:** *A gorgonian sea fan clings to a vertical wall in the deep clear seas around Tubbataha Reef National Marine Park, a remote atoll in the Sulu Sea.*

Plant life revolves mainly around the **tropical rainforest**, with **dipterocarp** trees, the tall giants of the forest, dominant in the lowland forests, and smaller tropical **oaks** taking over at higher altitudes. Below the tree canopy grow several species of pandanus, rattan, palms, vines and ferns. In the muddy estuaries and bays **mangroves** are quite common.

**Coral reefs** occur below the low-tide mark, with approximately 400 species of coral recorded in the Philippines. Healthy reefs are home to hundreds of species of fish, from the tiny striped **clownfish**, beautiful **butterflyfish** and **Moorish idols** to the huge **grouper**. Around the reefs that are surrounded by deep water it is common to encounter **barracuda**, **tuna** and **sharks**. In the deepest waters there are often **dolphins** and **whales**.

Many of the land animals are unfamiliar to visitors, although **macaques** are common. Palawan has a number of species familiar in other parts of Asia, such as the **otter** and **mouse deer**. Philippine endemic species include the

## PROTECTED AREAS

Some of the Philippines' most important (for conservation value) protected areas are as follows:

| Protected area | Location | Habitat |
|---|---|---|
| Mount Apo Natural Park | Southern Mindanao | Rainforest |
| Mount Kitanglad Range Natural Park | Northern Mindanao | Rainforest |
| Northern Sierra Madre Natural Park | Northern Luzon | Rainforest |
| Subic–Bataan Natural Park | Central Luzon | Rainforest and mangroves |
| Mount Pulag National Park | Northern Luzon | Pine and mossy forests |
| Mount Kanlaon Natural Park | Negros, Visayas | Rainforest |
| Siargao Island Protected Landscapes and Seascapes | Northern Mindanao | Rainforest remnants, mangroves, coastal scenery |
| Batanes Islands Protected Landscapes and Seascapes | Northern Luzon | Coastal cliffs and rocks, rainforest remnants |
| Agusan Marsh Wildlife Sanctuary | Central Mindanao | Freshwater marsh |
| Tubbataha Reef National Marine Park | Palawan | Coral reefs and atolls |
| Apo Reef Marine Natural Park | Mindoro | Coral reefs and atolls |
| Turtle Islands Marine Turtle Sanctuary | Tawi-Tawi | Coral islands |

**tamaraw**, a wild buffalo that survives only on Mindoro, as well as several species of deer. Apart from this, most of the mammals are rather small, consisting largely of **bats** and **rodents**.

The Philippines' most famous bird is undoubtedly the **Philippine eagle**, the world's second-largest raptor. It lives in the rainforests, but loss of habitat has brought it close to extinction. It survives in Mindanao, Luzon, Samar and Leyte.

## Conservation

Although the country had one of the world's first national park systems, set up during the American colonial period, since independence the rapid population growth and lack of concern for the environment have led to devastation. Since World War II, for example, 90 per cent of lowland forests have been lost, with only those in the mountains surviving. At sea, areas of coral reefs have been ruined by dynamite and cyanide fishing. As a result many species are endangered, soil erosion has become severe, water supplies are at risk, and fisheries have been decimated.

In the 1990s a major international initiative to promote conservation in the Philippines was launched. Consisting of two huge projects funded by the World Bank and European Union, a new protected areas system was launched, 20 of the most important surviving wild areas receiving close protection, along with better funding for management of many areas left over from the old system. Unfortunately, both funding bodies pulled out after their first five- and seven-year phases, leaving much of the conservation programme in limbo. Today, however, many projects continue using local expertise and overseas funding. An example of this is work carried out by the US organization Conservation International, which has led to the protection of over 4000km² of lowland rainforest along Luzon's northeastern coast.

**Below:** At barely 8cm (3 in) the Philippine tarsier is one of the world's smallest primates.

Also known as Malayo-Polynesians, these are the ancestors of most of the inhabitants of Southeast Asia and the Pacific, as far east as Easter Island. Their origins have been greatly disputed, with early theories arguing they came from the islands of today's central and eastern Indonesia, the Sundas. However, most anthropologists now believe they originated in either Taiwan or southern China. About 5000 years ago they started to migrate southwards, either by boat from Taiwan to the Philippines and thence west into Indonesia and Malaysia, and east into the Pacific, or possibly following the coast from China to Indochina and archipelagic Southeast Asia, then to the Pacific. They are the ancestors of today's Filipinos.

**Below:** *An exhibit of a* Hagabi *(clan bench) as used by the Ifugao people, Northern Luzon.*

## HISTORY IN BRIEF
### Prehistory
The earliest signs of human life go back 750,000 years, to finds made in the Cagayan Valley in the far north. It is likely, however, that these were formed by *Homo erectus*, the predecessor of *Homo sapiens*. The first signs of the latter date to 30,000–50,000 years ago, mainly from the **Tabon Caves** in Palawan. It is believed that they were related to today's **Negritos**, a tribal group that continues to live in the forests and mountains of some parts of the country.

About 5000 years ago the islands received a wave of immigration: **Austronesian** peoples, probably travelling from their homeland in southern China and/or Taiwan. They occupied the whole country and then fanned out, travelling east and west to populate Southeast Asia and much of the Pacific. Later there were more, smaller immigrations, mostly **Malays** coming in from Borneo.

### The Early Philippines
No central power arose to make the Philippines a single country. Instead, the people lived in autonomous clusters of villages, or ***barangays***, each with its own chieftain. In time, some places became important trading centres, often outposts of the Indianized empires of Southeast Asia. These places became part of the developing Asian maritime trade routes very early on.

By the 10th century, Filipino merchants were sailing to

China for business; ships from China's Song and Yuan dynasties (AD960–1368) traded extensively with the Philippines. Large finds of Chinese pottery and coins indicate that the main Philippine trading centres were at **Butuan** (on the north coast of Mindanao), **Cebu**, **Tondo** (a district in today's Manila) and the **Sulu Islands**.

From the 13th century, **Arab missionaries** began arriving in the Sulu Islands on Chinese ships, starting the Islamization of the south-west. Sulu's first Islamic sultanate was established in 1450 under **Sayyid Abu Bakr**, a refugee prince from Sumatra. Islam then spread northwards into Mindanao.

**Above:** *Raha Humabon, chief of Cebu, is christened by Magellan, in the Philippines' first baptism.*

At this time **Tondo**, on the northern shore of the Pasig River roughly in the area of today's Binondo district of Manila, came under the control of the Brunei empire. Many Malays and Chinese settled here, forming the nucleus of modern Manila's Chinatown. Brunei also established a settlement on the southern shore of the Pasig, right at the river's mouth, which was possibly called **Maynilad**, the predecessor of today's Manila.

## The Arrival of the Spanish

Ferdinand Magellan, a Portuguese working in the service of Spain, left Spain in 1519, intent on finding a route to the Spice Islands. On 16 March 1521 he and his men arrived off the coast of Samar. Their first landfall was on **Homonhon**, an island just south of Samar. From here they sailed to **Limasawa**, and then to Cebu, where they arrived on 7 April 1521. The chief of Cebu, **Raha Humabon**, was remarkably friendly, and within days Magellan had baptized him and many of his followers.

Magellan then made a fatal error. A dispute arose with Humabon's neighbour, **Lapu-Lapu**, chief of **Mactan Island**, into which Magellan was drawn. In the resulting battle, on **27 April 1521**, Magellan was killed by Lapu-Lapu. Many of Magellan's officers were massacred by Humabon's men, the survivors fleeing aboard their ships. Over a year later, they returned to Spain, only 18 men out of the original 265.

Between 1523 and 1546 Spain sent three more expeditions, and by the 1550s the islands had become known

### FERDINAND MAGELLAN

A Portuguese adventurer, Magellan took part in the battle that captured the Malay port of Malacca for Portugal in 1511. He believed he could reach the Spice Islands of Indonesia from Europe by sailing westwards, but could not convince the Portuguese king to sponsor a test voyage. In 1518, he had more success with the Spanish king, and in 1519 set out with five ships from the Spanish port of San Lucar. Although he was killed in the Philippines and few of the crew survived, the voyage was a historic triumph. This was the first circumnavigation of the globe, proving the Earth to be round and that one could indeed reach the Spice Islands by sailing west.

**Opposite:** *Defensive walls around Intramuros, Manila's historic Spanish-era walled city.*

as **Islas Filipinas**, in honour of King Philip II of Spain. But not until 1565 and an expedition led by **Miguel de Legaspi** did Spain start to gain a hold on the Philippines. In that year Legaspi set up the first permanent Spanish settlement in Cebu, though fears of an attack by the Portuguese led him to move to Panay.

In the following year, the Spanish decided to attack Manila. An invasion force arrived in May 1570, and after some initial friendly contact a fight started, as a result of which Manila burned. Despite their victory, the Spanish withdrew to Panay. They returned in May 1571, and this time the Malay leaders surrendered. The Spanish city of Manila was born. From being a simple wooden settlement, attacks by the Chinese pirate **Li Mahong** and repeated fires led to its development as a highly fortified stone city, very similar to the **Intramuros** that we see today.

## HISTORICAL CALENDAR

**circa 60,000–20,000BC** Man inhabits Tabon Caves, Palawan.
**c AD960** Chinese goods begin to appear in the Philippines.
**c1100** Chinese colonies are founded along the coasts.
**c1200** Islam starts to filter into the far south of the Philippines.
**1521** Ferdinand Magellan arrives in the Philippines.
**1565** Miguel Lopez de Legaspi arrives in Cebu and sets up first permanent Spanish settlement.
**1571** Legaspi takes possession of Manila and makes it the capital of the Philippines.
**1762–4** British occupy Manila.
**1834** Manila opened to world trade.
**1861** Birth of José Rizal.
**1887** Rizal's novel, *Noli me Tangere*, published in Berlin.
**1892** Andres Bonifacio founds the Katipunan, dedicated to ending Spanish rule.

**1896, August** Bonifacio starts the Philippine Revolution.
**1896, December** José Rizal is executed.
**1898, April** The US Congress declares war on Spain.
**1898, 12 June** The Philippines declares independence.
**1898, August** Spain surrenders Manila to the USA.
**1898, December** In the Treaty of Paris, the USA buys the Philippines from Spain.
**1899** The Philippine–American War breaks out.
**1902** Resistance to American rule ends.
**1935** The Commonwealth of the Philippines is inaugurated.
**1941** Japan attacks.
**1942** US–Filipino forces surrender to the Japanese.
**1944** General MacArthur leads the American landings on Leyte.
**1945** Japanese occupation ends.

**1946, 4 July** The country gains independence.
**1972** President Marcos declares martial law.
**1983** Opposition leader Benigno Aquino is assassinated.
**1986, 7 Feb** A snap election sees Marcos 're-elected'.
**1986, 25 Feb** The People's Power Revolution deposes Marcos. Corazon Aquino becomes president.
**1998, 12 June** Centennial celebrations for the country's declaration of independence.
**2001** President Joseph Estrada indicted for corruption, removed from office and replaced by vice-president Gloria Macapagal-Arroyo.
**2007** Joseph Estrada tried and found guilty of corruption, but immediately pardoned by President Macapagal-Arroyo, and released.

## Spanish Rule

The Spanish extended their influence throughout lowland Luzon and the Visayas. Catholic priests were able to convert the Filipinos in their tens of thousands, greatly easing the spread of Spanish control. To govern the population, the many scattered settlements were compressed into towns and villages built around a church. The Spanish religious authorities also took it upon themselves to destroy everything they could of the pre-Hispanic era. They did a very thorough job, wiping out records of life before their arrival and completely doing away with the native alphabet – a script similar in appearance to other non-Roman alphabets still in use in parts of South and Southeast Asia today.

With regard to trade, one of the most famous developments was the **Manila Galleons**, the annual sailing of a ship from Manila to Acapulco in Mexico, loaded up with trade goods and treasure. The annual event began early in the city's life and continued until 1815, making a few people immensely rich, though it was of no benefit to the country as a whole. Ironically, the success of trade between Manila and other parts of East Asia depended on the **Chinese community**. They became an essential part of the economy, but the Spanish always mistrusted them. As a result, the Chinese were never allowed into Intramuros and they were forced to live on the banks of the Pasig River, within range of the walled city's guns.

### THE MANILA GALLEONS (1565–1815)

For 250 years the Spanish of the Philippines ran the only regular shipping service across the Pacific. Each year two galleons, one each heading east and west, travelled between Manila and Acapulco. The ship leaving Manila would carry trade goods from the Philippines, Southeast Asia and China, paid for by the returning ship in Mexican silver dollars. The round trip took about 200 days. The trade made fortunes for a small number of Manila Spaniards, but went into decline in the late 18th century following the foundation of the Royal Philippine Company, which shipped goods directly to Spain via the Cape of Good Hope.

### THE ENCOMIENDA SYSTEM

Set up in the earliest days of Spanish rule, this was the awarding of parcels of land, including all the people on it, to men who had served the Spanish crown. The owner of an *encomienda* could exact taxes and loyalty from the people on 'his' land, and had to give protection in return. However, this was usually abused, leading to exploitation of the local people. It was the start of absentee landlordism, with the establishment of huge estates and the concentration of land, and hence power, into a few hands. Such land ownership patterns continue today, despite government's claims to be supporting land reform.

## JOSÉ RIZAL (1861–96)

Seen today as the founding father of the nation, his statue can be seen in the centre of almost every town and city. Born in Calamba close to the southern shore of Laguna de Bay, he studied medicine in Manila and later in Madrid, London, Heidelberg, Paris and Berlin, returning to the Philippines in 1892. While in Europe he wrote extensively about Spanish oppression in the Philippines, including his two books *Noli me Tangere* and *El Filibusterismo*. Back in the Philippines he founded a pro-democracy movement, Liga Filipina, and was quickly exiled to Mindanao. When the revolution broke out in 1896 he was brought back to Manila for trial, and was executed on 30 December 1896.

## Rebellion and the Independence Movement

From the earliest days of Spain's occupation, rebellions were common. The most famous of the early uprisings were those in the far north, led by husband and wife **Diego** and **Gabriela Silang**, but a more truly successful rebellion occurred on Bohol. In 1744 **Francisco Dagohoy** succeeded in wresting independence for the island, something which lasted until 1829 when the Spanish finally succeeded in re-invading.

During the 19th century European liberal ideas of democracy spread to the Philippines via Filipinos who had studied in Europe. These men campaigned for democracy at home, one of the foremost of whom was **José Rizal** (1861–96). His two novels *Noli me Tangere* (meaning 'Don't Touch Me') and *El Filibusterismo* (meaning 'Subversion') exposed the corruption of the Spanish Philippine government and predicted a revolution. His books were banned in the Philippines, and after returning home he was exiled to Mindanao.

While Rizal favoured peaceful change, others were for open rebellion. One, **Andres Bonifacio**, formed

the **Katipunan** in 1892, an organization dedicated to the violent overthrow of the Spanish. Its membership grew by tens of thousands, and when its secret network was discovered in 1896 Bonifacio launched the revolution. The colonial government accused Rizal of involvement and executed him on the edge of what is now Rizal Park, just outside Intramuros, on 30 December 1896. The **Philippine Revolution** had its greatest martyr.

Fighting went on for several months, during which time an internal struggle broke out within the Katipunan, resulting in the execution of Bonifacio, and the emergence of a new leader, **Emilio Aguinaldo**. The Spanish were unable to put the revolution down, but neither could the Filipinos defeat the Spanish. At the end of

**Left:** *The capture of General Emilio Aguinaldo, first president of the Philippine Republic, by American troops brought to an end resistance to American rule.*
**Opposite:** *A statue of Gabriela Silang, first heroine of the Philippine independence move-ment, stands before the Stock Exchange Tower in Makati.*

### HEROES OF THE REVOLUTION

There is a long roll call of people who played a major part in the Philippine Revolution against Spanish rule. Some of the main individuals were as follows:
**Apolinario Mabini:** the brains of the revolution who drafted the first constitution.
**Emilio Aguinaldo:** a leading general in the revolution, who became the first president of the new republic, declared on 12 June 1898.
**José Rizal:** an intellectual whose writings stirred the country towards independence. He was executed by the Spanish.
**Andres Bonifacio:** a leading general who set up the Katipunan in 1892 and launched the revolution in 1896.
**Antonio Luna:** leading general, murdered by his own men.
**Emilio Jacinto:** founder of the Katipunan and a leading commander.

1897 a truce was finally agreed, with the leaders of the revolution going into exile in Hong Kong.

Peace did not last long, however, due in part to the out-break of the **Spanish–American War**, resulting from a dispute over Cuba. The USA made plans to invade the Philippines and encouraged the exiles to return home. In May 1898, combined American and Filipino forces laid siege to Manila, and on **12 June 1898** the new Philippine government declared independence from Spain. Freedom was short-lived. The Spanish agreed to surrender, but only to the Americans and only with a face-saving mock battle that excluded the Filipino forces. In this way the Americans took Manila on 13 August 1898, with Aguinaldo and his men frozen out.

Any doubts over the USA's intentions were dispelled by the **Treaty of Paris**, signed in December 1898, in which the USA bought the Philippines from Spain for US$20 million. The Filipinos were soon at war with their new masters, but it was a one-sided fight that ended in Aguinaldo's capture.

**Above:** *Ruins litter Corregidor, the island fortress guarding the entrance to Manila Bay. They stand as silent testament to the battles that have raged around it in the past.*

## American Colonial Rule

The early years of the USA's occupation were marked by the occasional brutal suppression of an uprising, but overall the government grew relatively benign. The elite of Philippine society were easily persuaded to co-operate and by the 1910s a US-style congress was established that was largely controlled by wealthy Filipinos, though its powers could be vetoed by the American governor.

The possibility of total independence was raised as early as 1916, but a change in US policy in the early 1920s led to an indefinite delay in the process. However, by early 1933 it had been agreed that the Philippines would pass through a commonwealth phase, starting in 1935 and culminating in full independence on 4 July 1946. On 8 February 1935 the Commonwealth of the Philippines was inaugurated with **Manuel Quezon** as president.

## World War II

Preparations for full independence were smashed in December 1941 when the Japanese bombed Pearl Harbor. Within hours American bases in the Philippines were bombed and before year's end, Manila. In December Japanese forces landed in many places in the Philippines. The outnumbered American forces, along with members of the Philippine government, retreated to **Corregidor Island** and the **Bataan Peninsula** in the mouth of Manila Bay. The Japanese entered Manila on 2 January 1942.

The besieged US–Filipino force held out for several months, though once Manuel Quezon and the US commander, **Douglas MacArthur**, had been ordered to leave, resistance weakened. Bataan surrendered in April 1942, followed by Corregidor in May.

### THE HUKBALAHAP

During the Japanese occupation there was a very active resistance movement. Several guerrilla groups were able to control large territories, running them on socialist lines and bringing about extensive land reform. The largest of these groups was the Hukbalahap, a communist organization which controlled parts of northern and central Luzon. With liberation in 1945, the Huk were reluctant to give up their territory and the land reform they had achieved, and so were outlawed and repressed. They returned to guerrilla activities and were not finally defeated until the mid-1950s.

There followed three years of Japanese rule, characterized by continual guerrilla warfare against the occupiers; but by 1944 the Americans were returning. On **20 October 1944**, US forces under MacArthur landed on **Red Beach** on the east coast of Leyte. Further landings on Mindoro in December and then in the Lingayen Gulf north of Manila in January 1945 brought the USA to within striking distance of the capital. After heavy fighting Manila fell on 3 February 1945.

## Independence

Despite the war the country received full independence on 4 July 1946, as planned. The first president of the new republic was **Manuel Roxas**.

Since then, the Philippines has maintained its US-inspired democracy, one closely allied with the USA. The country became a major bastion in the West's fight against the spread of communism, numerous American bases being maintained across the country. The most important were the naval base at **Subic Bay** and the nearby **Clark Airforce Base**, both of which saw extensive service during the Vietnam War. The presence of the US military became a sovereignty issue, and when the 1991 eruption of **Mount Pinatubo** caused massive damage to Subic and Clark it became relatively simple for the Philippine Congress to ask the Americans to leave. The USA pulled out in 1992.

### HEY, JOE!

Most visitors will hear this cry as they walk along the streets. To many Filipinos every Westerner is called Joe, a leftover from the American 'GI Joe' days, and apparently they believe it appropriate to yell 'Hey, Joe!' across the street at you. This phenomenon is especially prevalent in areas where foreigners are uncommon, and is something that is simply to be tolerated. In a few areas, such as Camiguin Island, the call has been modernized to the far nicer 'Hello, friend!'

**Left:** *At the village of Bacolor, near San Fernando, Pampanga province, houses buried up to their eaves in ash bear witness to the immensity of the lahar flows that poured down the slopes of Mount Pinatubo in the wake of its June 1991 eruption.*

## THE NEW PEOPLE'S ARMY

The New People's Army (NPA) is the military wing of the Communist Party of the Philippines, and was formed in 1969 out of the remains of the Hukbalahap, a guerilla group that had fought the Japanese occupation during World War II. The NPA rose to a peak in the 1980s, when it had 25,000 men and controlled large areas of the Philippine countryside. In the 1990s, President Fidel Ramos made a peace deal with the NPA, since which it has been much less active. Internal struggles followed, resulting in the deaths of many followers. Today the NPA continues low-level terrorist activity, and consists of about 8000 fighters.

For most of the post-war period the Philippines has remained democratic. One major hiccup, however, was the Marcos dictatorship. **Ferdinand Marcos** was elected president in 1965 on a wave of optimism that he would provide a fairer distribution of the country's wealth. He was popular for the first few years, but when he declared martial law in 1972 it served only to maintain his grip on power. The next few years were marked by oppression, corruption and a massive siphoning off of the country's wealth.

By the early 1980s the country was nearly bankrupt, and when **Benigno Aquino**, a popular opposition politician, was assassinated in 1983, literally as he was stepping off an airplane at Manila Airport upon his return from exile, the end was near for Marcos. An election in February 1986 saw all the opposition parties give their support to Aquino's widow **Corazon Aquino** in a joint move to push Marcos out. The vote clearly went in favour of Aquino, but Marcos claimed victory and held onto power.

A military coup followed but failed, and as army units loyal to Marcos moved to attack the rebels, the Archbishop of Manila, **Cardinal Jaime Sin**, called on all the people of Manila to come to their protection. Thousands of people turned out, blocking the path of the goverment forces and daring them to open fire on unarmed civilians. The US flew Marcos out to exile, and the **People's Power Revolution** triumphed. Corazon Aquino became the next president.

**Right:** *The annual Independence Day celebrations, held on 12 June in Manila, are a reminder of the country's long struggle for self-determination.*

A new constitution was written and the country gradually put back on its feet. But Aquino was not a skilled leader. She failed to tackle many of the underlying causes of poverty and was unable to stimulate the economy. Discontent soared, leading to numerous insurrections. By the late 1980s the communist **New People's Army** (NPA) controlled large parts of the countryside, especially on Mindanao. On this island too, Islamic separatists, mainly the **Moro National Liberation Front** (MNLF), controlled large areas.

In 1992 an election gave the presidency to **Fidel Ramos**, who made peace deals with the NPA and MNLF, and started a programme of industrialization and improved education. His approach began to bear fruit, the country's economy growing well until the downturn in the late 1990s in the economies of much of East Asia also badly hit Philippine development. In 1998 Ramos was replaced by **Joseph Estrada**, a film star who promised to bring wealth to the masses. He proved to be hugely corrupt, and in 2001 was deposed, replaced by his vice-president, Gloria Macapagal-Arroyo. Estrada was eventually tried and found guilty of corruption in 2007, but was immediately pardoned by President Macapagal-Arroyo and released from prison.

The Islamic insurgency in the far south continues, led by two groups, Abu Sayyaf and the Moro Islamic Liberation Front (MILF). Abu Sayyaf in particular has carried out some brutal terrorist attacks, including the 2004 sinking of a ferry.

**Above:** *The Philippine flag, decorated with three stars arranged in an equilateral triangle and a shining sun at its centre, is a combination of various symbols used by the Katipunan during the Philippine Revolution.*

## GOVERNMENT AND ECONOMY
### Government and Politics

Since independence, the Philippines has been a **republic** with a national government modelled on American lines, including a powerful elected **President** and a bicameral **Congress**. Congress's upper house, the **Senate,** consists of 24 senators, while the lower house, the **House of Representatives**, has up to 250 members. The president is elected every six years, and since the Marcos era, has been allowed

**ECONOMIC INDICATORS**

- **Gross Domestic Product (GDP):** US$325 billion
- **GDP annual growth rate:** 0.9%
- **Per capita GDP:** US$3300
- **Annual inflation rate:** 3.2%
- **Exports:** US$37.2 billion
- **Current account balance:** US$8.16 billion

**Right:** *The houses of workers at a seaweed farm stand in the shallows over Arena Reef.*

## DEMOGRAPHICS

- **Total population:**
- 98 million
- **Population annual growth rate:** 1.96%
- **Life expectancy:** 71
- **Birth rate:** 26.01 per 1000 population
- **Death rate:** 5.1 per 1000 population
- **Infant mortality rate:** 20.56 per 1000 live births
- **Fertility rate:** 3.27 children born per woman
- **Literacy rate:** 92.6%
- **Urban population:** 65%

## LOCAL GOVERNMENT

Below national government are three tiers of local government: provincial, municipal and *barangay*. The elected officials of the provincial government consist of the provincial governor and board members, the latter the province's elected assembly. Each province is divided into municipalities, each with an elected mayor and an elected assembly known as the *sanguniang*. Each municipality is divided into *barangays* – rural villages or urban districts – governed by an elected *barangay* captain and council. The *barangay* officials are elected every five years; the provincial and municipal representatives every three.

one term of office. The senators are also elected every six years, half of the 24 standing in a national election every three years. Members of the House of Representatives are elected every three years, each candidate standing as a regional representative and eligible to sit for up to three terms. The number of representatives each region is allowed to send to Congress depends on the local population.

There is quite an array of political parties, many of which operate as coalitions, particularly at election time. The most important include Lakas-Kampi-CMD, Genuine Opposition, the Nationalist People's Coalition (NPC), and the Democratic Filipino Struggle (LDP). The strength of individual personalities is critical, often more so than party policies.

Unlike the USA, the Philippines is not a federal nation. The country is divided into 15 major **regions** and below that into 79 **provinces**. Each province is divided into **municipalities**, centred on a major town or city. Below the municipal level comes the ***barangay***, which in the countryside usually equates to a single village, but which in an urban setting is usually one district or ward of a town or city. All members of local government are elected.

## Economy

Throughout the early 1990s, the Philippine economy began to recover well from the devastation caused by the years of the Marcos dictatorship. The country even weathered the Asian financial crisis of the late 1990s reasonably well, though things went downhill for a while under the presidency of Joseph Estrada. Since then, however, the economy has continued to recover, its growth rate frequently outperforming many of its neighbours, despite the global economic recession.

Although **industry** has developed over the past few years – centred mainly around Manila and Cebu City and producing processed foods, clothing and electrical goods – the country depends heavily on services and the primary products of agriculture and mining. The Philippines is a major mineral producer, particularly rich in gold and copper. For both metals the country is the largest producer in Southeast Asia, and in the top ten worldwide.

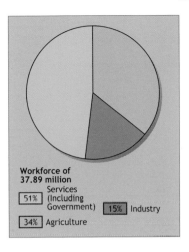

Workforce of
37.89 million
51% Services (Including Government)
15% Industry
34% Agriculture

Other important minerals are silver and chromite, while zinc, manganese, iron and cobalt are also present in small quantities. The search for oil has so far had limited success, though gas has been found, mainly in the Malampaya region of Palawan.

The growing service industry has pushed **agriculture** into second place as the country's main employer. Nevertheless, it is critical to rural employment. The principal agricultural products are rice, corn (maize), sugar cane, pineapples, coconuts (including copra) and bananas. A number of these crops are produced on small family-owned holdings, but most of them come from large estates.

Remittances sent from the many Filipinos working overseas are also an important factor in the economy. Although the cost of living is low, **poverty** is still widespread, with incomes in rural areas as low as US$40 per month. One of the problems that has persisted since the Spanish era is the unequal distribution of land, with **huge estates** concentrated into a few hands, leaving a large number of people with no secure tenure anywhere. The government's long-term failure to tackle this inequality is one of the major causes of the discontent and communist rebellions that have simmered since independence.

## UBIQUITOUS RICE

Rice is the main staple for almost all Filipinos, each person eating about 100kg (220lb) per year, accounting for about 41% of their calorie intake. The crop accounts for 4.27 million hectares (10 million acres), half of it irrigated, about a third of the country's total farmland. About 15 million tonnes are harvested annually, insufficient to feed the population. As a result, the Philippines is one of the world's biggest rice importers. The International Rice Research Institute (IRRI), near Los Banos, is in a constant race to find ways to improve productivity to keep up with growing needs, not just for the Philippines, but globally.

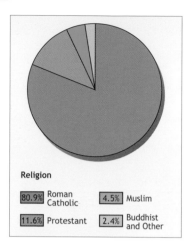

**Religion**

| | | | |
|---|---|---|---|
| 80.9% | Roman Catholic | 4.5% | Muslim |
| 11.6% | Protestant | 2.4% | Buddhist and Other |

## THE PEOPLE

The Filipinos of today are a curious blend of East and West, showing strong Malay, Chinese, Spanish and American inputs. While the first has laid the basic groundwork in terms of the people's physical appearance, temperament and main language structure, influences from the other three have been absorbed: nothing foreign has been rejected, but taken in and adapted to local use.

The vast majority of today's Filipinos are descended from Austronesians who migrated from the north 5000 years ago, founding the Philippine, Malay and Polynesian peoples as they travelled and colonized. In many areas there is an overlay of more recent Malay immigrations, particularly in and around Panay.

A Spanish legacy takes the form of numerous phrases and words absorbed into the vernacular, most importantly in names of places and people. It is a similar story with the American influence, which has led Christian names, for example, to be pronounced in the anglicized manner even if given a Spanish spelling. Many aspects of urban lifestyle are also remnants of the American past, including a yearning for the 'American Dream'. There are still extensive family and business connections between the Philippines and the USA.

**PHILIPPINE ENGLISH**

While it is true to say that English is widely spoken across the Philippines, it is often used in ways that may not be familiar to visiting native speakers. For one thing, to many Filipinos the spoken vocabulary is often closer than normal to the written language, sometimes making their speech seem rather stiff and overly formal, something quite incongruous in an otherwise generally informal people.

**Opposite:** *A young fishing family sift through their nets for fish after a trawl along the sea shore; Siargao Island, Mindanao.* **Right:** *A brightly painted tricycle takes a school girl to class; Dumaguete, Negros Oriental.*

Another major American legacy is the widespread use of English. One of the country's two official languages, its teaching is compulsory in school and it is often the principal language in business and government. This tends to create a barrier to advancement for the poorer, less educated parts of society. Nevertheless, the visitor will find that even the poorest fisherman is able to make basic English conversation.

Few people, however, use English as their first language. There are said to be over 80 languages and dialects in the Philippines, though the vast majority speak one or more of the eight principal tongues: Tagalog, Ilocano, Pangasinan, Pampangan, Bicol, Cebuano, Waray-Waray and Ilongo (also called Hili-gaynon). With 30 per cent of the population speaking **Tagalog**, including those in the Manila area, this has become, in a standardized form called **Pilipino**, the other official national language.

## Daily Life

One of the most striking features of Philippine life is the prominence of women. While raising a family is a major goal for the great majority of Filipinos and Filipinas, as men and women are respectively called, this does not prevent women achieving senior positions and success in government and business. That this is possible is partly due to the strength of the extended family, young women being freed to work by grandparents who can look after children. It is also due to the inequality in society that enables wealthier people to employ those from the poorer levels of society as house- and child-minders on low wages.

The strength of the extended family is important in allowing poor families, especially in the countryside, collectively to make a living. In wealthier families strong ties of kinship make it possible for family members to help each other succeed.

### THE JEEPNEY

The jeepney is the ubiquitous form of public transport, unique to the Philippines. It was born at the end of World War II out of a desperate shortage of public transport vehicles and an excess of US military jeeps. Workshops sprang up to lengthen the jeeps' chassis, fit benches down the sides and put a roof over the top. Today they still dominate the roads, though they have come some way since 1945, and not just the padding on the benches. Painted and decorated with flamboyant designs, slogans and even statuettes, many are mobile works of pop art. Most are also equipped with very powerful hi-fi systems, used to considerable effect, and a few are even decorated with flashing lights.

**Top:** *On Good Friday penitents allow themselves to be nailed to a cross.* **Below:** *An Ifugao village, Cordillera Central.*

The problem of finding sufficient work in the Philippines has led many to work overseas. Filipinas are frequently seen in domestic work in Hong Kong and other wealthy Asian countries, while men are common in the oil industry of the Middle East and the world's merchant shipping. Their remittances are an important contribution to maintaining families back home.

The need to generate as many workers as possible in a poor family, along with a genuine love of children and a Roman Catholic opposition to birth control, has created a rapidly growing population. Already standing at 98 million, the population's annual growth rate is about 1.96 per cent, one of the highest in Asia, and shows little sign of slowing down. To date, only the educated classes have recognized the need to limit family size.

**Religion** plays a central part in daily life. Ninety per cent of the population is Christian, 5 per cent Muslim and the remainder a mixture of Buddhist and animist. Of the Christians 92 per cent are Roman Catholic, 8 per cent Protestant. There are a couple of home-grown Christian groups, notably Iglesia ni Cristo, a nationalistic protestant group, and the Philippine Independent Church, a Catholic body. Attendance of mass and personal prayer are common, often combined with some folk superstitions, a remnant of pre-Christian days.

## Ethnic and Tribal Groups

About 10 per cent of the population belongs to one of the country's many ethnic minorities, about half of these **Muslims** in the far south. Of the remainder, an important element are the **Negritos**, often called by a variety of names, such as Aeta or Agta. Now numbering less than 15,000 they are mainly scattered across Panay and Luzon. They prefer to live in remote forests and mountains, and are all that remains of the country's first inhabitants.

Other important groups, most of them numerically stronger than the Negritos, include the Ifugao, Bontoc, Kalinga, Mangyan, T'boli, Manobo, Tausug, Badjao and Tagbanua. The first three live in the Cordillera Central of northern Luzon. Warlike people that used to be headhunters, they have traditionally been resistant to outside control and were only integrated into the Philippines during Amer-

| MAIN TRIBAL OR ETHNIC MINORITIES | |
|---|---|
| **Name** | **Location(s)** |
| Negritos (Aeta, Agta, Ati, Ata, Ita, Dumagat) | Various mountainous regions of Luzon, Panay and Negros |
| Ilocano | Northern Luzon |
| Apayao | Northern Luzon |
| Kalinga | Cordillera Central, in Northern Luzon |
| Bontoc | Cordillera Central, in Northern Luzon |
| Ifugao | Cordillera Central, in Northern Luzon |
| Mangyan (Iraya, Alangan, Tadyawan, Buhid, Hanunoo) | Mindoro |
| Manobo | Eastern and Central Mindanao |
| Bagobo | Southern Mindanao |
| Tasaday | Southern Mindanao |
| T'boli | Southern Mindanao |
| Mandaya | Southern Mindanao |
| Maranao | Western Mindanao |
| Samal | Western Mindanao |
| Subanon | Western Mindanao |
| Yakan | Western Mindanao and Basilan Island |
| Tausug | Sulu Islands |
| Badjao | Sulu Islands and Palawan |
| Tagbanua | Palawan (especially Calamian Islands) |
| Batak | Palawan |
| Tau't Batu | Palawan |
| Pala'wan | Palawan |
| Jama Mapun | Southern Palawan |

ican rule. It was the **Ifugao** who 2000 years ago built the stupendous rice terraces on the hills around Banaue. The **Mangyan** are the main inhabitants of Mindoro, living mostly in the interior. A large group, they are subdivided, those in the north and the south speaking mutually incomprehensible languages. The **Manobo** live scattered across eastern Mindanao and the **T'boli** live in the southwestern part of this island, while the **Tausug** are the main Muslim inhabitants of the Sulu Islands. The **Badjao** live on the Sulu Islands and Palawan, on boats or in houses built on stilts above water. They rarely come onto land, except to be buried. The **Tagbanua** are a rather shy farming group concentrated mostly in northern Palawan.

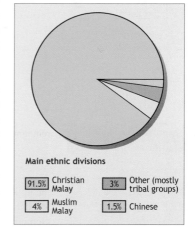

**Main ethnic divisions**

91.5% Christian Malay
4% Muslim Malay
3% Other (mostly tribal groups)
1.5% Chinese

## FAVOURITE DISHES

Filipino food is a blend of Malay, Chinese, Spanish and American. Some of the best-known traditional dishes are:
*Adobo* • Chicken, pork or squid cooked in a sauce of garlic, vinegar, pepper and salt.
*Balut* • A lightly boiled duck's egg containing a partially formed embryo.
*Bangus* • Milkfish, a small fish cooked in a variety of ways.
*Batchoy* • Meats, often also intestines, in a noodle soup.
*Bihon* • Fried rice noodles.
*Halo-halo* • A sweet dessert made of beans and nuts, usually served on a bed of ice.
*Kare-kare* • Not a curry, but a beef stew, often with finely ground peanuts and rice.
*Lapu-lapu* • Grouper, a large fish cooked in various ways.
*Lechon* • Young pig, usually roasted on a spit.
*Lumpia* • Large spring rolls.
*Mami* • Noodle soup.
*Pancit Canton* and *Pancit Guisado* • Fried noodles with meat and vegetables.
*Sinigang* • A sour vegetable soup containing fish or pork.
*Siopao* • A large doughy bun filled with chicken or pork.
Various dim sum are available in some Chinese restaurants, while American fast-food restaurants abound.

**Opposite:** *Dancing at Dinagyang Festival, held annually in Iloilo, largest city on Panay.*
**Right:** *Barbecued chicken and other food stalls during a food festival in Iloilo.*

## Festivals

Festivals are a major part of Philippine life, and always a great spectacle for the visitor. Every city, town and village holds at least one festival every year, usually related to such dates as the 'birthday' of the local patron saint or other religious icon, a harvest thanksgiving for the main local agricultural crop, a historical or mythological anniversary, or a combination of all these. One thing is for sure: this is the annual excuse for the locals to forget their troubles and really let their hair down. Drunkenness, loud music and dancing are essential parts of every festival, though there is usually a more serious religious element, such as a blessing or a special mass. Often there are also parades and competitions, carried out with varying degrees of seriousness. Beauty contests are another popular feature of Philippine life.

Much more serious are the Independence Day parades that occur in Manila on 12 June each year, marking the anniversary of the Declaration of Independence from Spain. A big event, this is mainly a chance for the military to show off its firepower.

## Arts and Handicrafts

With its long history of exposure to the West, a large proportion of Philippine art and entertainment is in the European style. This is perhaps most obvious in popular music, where rock, both foreign and home grown, is the

### BAGUIO: THE FRUIT AND VEG CAPITAL

At certain times of year you can see street vendors walking through the traffic jams in Manila selling strawberries. Where does this temperate fruit grow in a tropical country? In the mountains of the Cordillera Central. North of Baguio terraced hillsides are covered with fruit and vegetable farms producing not just strawberries, but also carrots, tomatoes, cabbages and potatoes. A walk through Baguio's market reveals the diversity of these mountains' products, and whenever you eat such vegetables in the Philippines you can be reasonably sure that they came from the Baguio region.

staple. Filipinos excel as musicians, and there are a large number of bands – producing both their own music and cover versions of famous songs – working as hotel entertainers right across Asia.

However, since independence many Filipino artists have searched for native roots, something made difficult by the long Spanish rule. Slowly, old themes have re-emerged, particularly in the well-established professional **dance** groups, which are an interesting amalgam of Spanish, Malay and tribal. This is most easily seen in the free weekend performances in Intramuros and Rizal Park. Even the orchestras that accompany the dancers reflect the mixed influence, as they switch between Spanish guitars and Malay percussion instruments.

**Handicrafts** have become a major product, especially among some of the tribal groups, who have found a new livelihood as a result. Produced at least in part for tourism, domestic as well as international, the products are often of high quality and reflect some of the traditional beliefs and skills of the tribal people. **Woodcarvings** of traditional figures are common, along with **basketry** products such as fruit bowls and floor mats. Patterned woven fabics are produced in styles similar to Indonesian **ikats**, while the Muslims of the southwest have colourful dyed fabrics. Interestingly, these handicrafts are slowly appearing in craft shops around the world.

### FRUIT

Fruit vendors usually stock apples, oranges and bananas, and also tropical fruits:
**Durian:** A large fruit with a thick, spiny shell, a pungent smell and very sweet taste.
**Jackfruit:** Similar to durian, but with a smoother, dark green skin. Flesh is yellow.
**Kalamansi:** A small lime-like fruit, often used in lemon tea.
**Lanzones:** About the size of a cherry. The skin is peeled off to reveal translucent flesh.
**Mango:** Usually yellow, with a rich sweet taste.
**Mangosteen:** Very thick, dark purple skin; pearly white segments with sweet-sour taste.
**Rambutan:** Egg-shaped with a dry, red, spikey skin and translucent flesh.

# 2
# Metro Manila

Created in the 1970s by the merging of eight cities and nine towns, Metropolitan Manila is the capital of the Philippines – a sprawling city of over 12 million people. For Filipinos in other parts of the country this is El Dorado, constantly drawing them in from the poor countryside. The result is an overcrowded metropolis that is constantly expanding. Traffic congestion and air pollution are problems, and can make Manila rather daunting for the first-time visitor. It is, however, a fascinating place, one that is worth spending time exploring and getting to know.

The section of the city that is **Manila** itself consists of a north–south orientated rectangle on the shore of **Manila Bay**, reaching from the port area north of the **Pasig River** south to the border with Pasay City, in the vicinity of the Philippine International Convention Center. Here are **Chinatown** (where many of the city's Chinese businesses are concentrated), **Intramuros** (the original Spanish city), **Rizal Park** (the green oasis of the inner city) and **Ermita** and **Malate** districts (areas in which many visitors stay).

To the south lie **Pasay** and **Parañaque**, site of the international airport, while to the east is **Makati**, the main business district, home to international companies, chic shopping centres and hotels. This is the modern, wealthy face of Metro Manila. To the northeast is **Quezon City**, centre of the Philippine government. Many of the sightseeing areas are concentrated in the old parts of Manila. For shopping and entertainment, however, head for either Manila's Ermita and Malate, or Makati.

## DON'T MISS

** **Intramuros:** old Spanish walled city, founded 1571, at the mouth of the Pasig River.
** **Rizal Park:** a green swathe on the southern edge of Intramuros, enjoyable on Sundays.
** **Nayong Pilipino:** a cultural village showing the various architectural styles found across the Philippines.
* **Ayala Museum:** a good exhibition of dioramas tracing the history of the Philippines.
* **Corregidor Island:** a fortified island in the mouth of Manila Bay, fought over by the Spanish, Americans and Japanese.

**Opposite:** *Fountain outside the Peninsula Hotel, Makati, Metro Manila.*

## NORTH OF THE PASIG RIVER

This area is one of the most crowded parts of the city. It consists of numerous narrow shopping streets and jammed **markets**, which are well worth exploring for a taste of Manila life. There are also several **churches**, the massive **Chinese Cemetery** and the **Malacañang Palace**, home to Philippine presidents.

### Malacañang Palace ★

Situated on the north bank of the Pasig River, this ornate building was originally the home of a Spanish merchant. Early in the 19th century it became the residence of the Spanish and then American heads of government, and when the Philippines gained independence, their own presidents occupied the building. A museum in the palace can be toured but at present only by written arrangement seven days in advance; tel/fax: 02 784 4286, or write to The Director, Malacanang Museum, Kalayaan Hall, Malacanang, Manila (further updates about this at www.op.gov.ph/museum).

Metro Manila

### Quiapo Church and Market ★

Situated to the west of the Malacañang Palace is Quiapo Church. Down one side of it runs congested Quezon Boulevard, and to the west is a mass of crowded streets lined with shops and filled with market stalls. This market is always a lively and interesting place to visit. The church itself, on the other hand, is disappointingly modern, having been built only in 1899 and restored in 1935.

Its fame stems from what lies inside – the statue of the **Black Nazarene**. It is a statue of Jesus bearing a cross, whose wood has weathered in such a way that Jesus has turned almost black. It is said to have been made by an Aztec artist in Mexico, and then brought to Manila at some time in the 17th century. The statue is revered all over the Philippines, and on 9 January each year, on the **Festival of the Black Nazarene**, it is paraded through the streets of Quiapo surrounded by a tumultuous crowd.

**Above:** *The statue of the Black Nazarene struggles through a seething crowd in Quiapo, during the Festival of the Black Nazarene.*

## Chinatown ★

This fascinating area stretches more or less from Santa Cruz Church in the east to Binondo Church in the west. Escolta and Ongpin streets are the main shopping thoroughfares. Chinatown has been destroyed several times over the centuries, most recently in 1945. Today, it shows all the signs of having been rather hurriedly and cheaply rebuilt. Dilapidated and terribly overcrowded, it is nevertheless a lively and colourful place to visit, especially in the run-up to Chinese New Year, when the markets are even more crowded than usual.

## Chinese Cemetery ★

Further to the north is the Chinese Cemetery. This is not the kind of place one would normally recommend for a tour, but it is quite remarkable nonetheless. It is filled with tombs as big as houses, grandiose in both scale and decoration. The tombs are expressions of incredible wealth by their deceased Chinese occupants – some of them are even equipped with electricity and running water, not to mention stained-glass windows. The cemetery is also a peaceful escape from the furore of the city outside.

**MANILA BEFORE THE SPANISH**

A settlement, called Tundun and later Tondo, existed on the north bank of the Pasig River in the 9th century AD – an outpost of Srivijaya, an Indianized Southeast Asian empire. When the empire faded in the 11th century, Tondo gained independence and became heavily involved in trade with the Arabs and Chinese. From early in the 16th century Tondo formed part of the Brunei Empire, at which time another Brunei settlement was established at the mouth of the Pasig River, called **Maynilad**. At the time of the Spanish arrival in 1570, the chief of Tondo was **Raha Lakandula**, and that of Maynilad **Raha Soleiman**, both Muslims. It was these men who fought and then surrendered to the Spanish.

## SOUTH OF THE RIVER

This is the part of Manila that most visitors to the Philippines come to know well. Here lies the city's main historical landmark, **Intramuros**, and beyond are the districts of **Ermita** and **Malate**, Manila's main tourist area.

### Intramuros ★★

Meaning 'within the walls', this is the old walled city that was the seat of the Spanish colonial administration. Today, most of the city is a reconstruction, as much of the original was devastated in 1945. The walls that surround Intramuros are more or less intact, and it is possible to explore the ramparts in a number of areas. One of the most interesting parts is in the southwest corner, at the **Baluarte de San Diego**, a massive corner bastion built on the site of the first Spanish fortress. In the southeast corner is another impressive fortification, the **Baluarte de San Andres**.

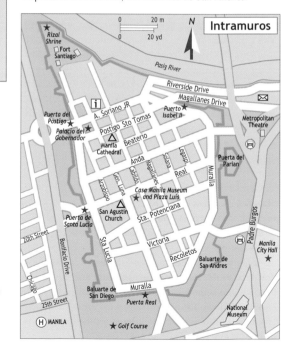

**Opposite:** *A rainbow spreads across a fountain in the ever popular Rizal Park, known by locals as Luneta.*

At the northern end is **Fort Santiago**, guarding the mouth of the Pasig River. Today it forms a pleasant garden and has a memorial to **José Rizal**, the national hero who was imprisoned here before his execution in 1896.

In the centre of Intramuros stands **Manila Cathedral**. The first church was erected here in 1581: the present cathedral is the sixth incarnation, rebuilt in 1958. To the south, on General Luna Street, is **San Agustin Church**, the oldest church in the country, built in 1571. Here is buried **Legaspi**, the Spanish founder of Manila. Miraculously this church has survived fire, earthquake and war. A small museum is attached to the church. Open 09:00–12:00 and 13:00–17:00 daily.

Across the road is the **Plaza Luis**, a complex of nine reconstructed buildings representing the designs of the different eras of Philippine architecture. Inside is **Casa Manila**, a museum designed to resemble a wealthy 19th-century home. Open 09:00–18:00 Tue–Sun.

## Rizal Park **

To the south of Intramuros, and separated from it by a golf course, is Rizal Park, popularly known as **Luneta**. This rectangular stretch of green is a popular place for Manila people to relax.

At the western end is **Rizal Monument**, erected close to where the national hero was executed. Behind stretches a **lagoon** with several fountains. To the north are the **Chinese Garden**, **Japanese Garden**, **Planetarium** and **open-air theatre**. The last of these is a good place to watch the free music or dance performances that take place on Sunday afternoons.

At the eastern end of the park is a skating rink, next to the **Department of Tourism**. To the north, on Padre Burgos St, is the **National Museum**, known for its exhibitions on pre-Hispanic Philippines, especially from the prehistoric era. Open 09:00–17:00 Tue–Sun.

## AMERICAN FORCES TAKE MANILA

By late July 1898 American and Filipino forces were laying siege to the Spanish in Manila. To avoid bloodshed, the American commander, Admiral George Dewey, entered into negotiations with the Spanish governor, Fermin Jaudenes. The latter agreed to surrender if Spanish honour could first be satisfied with a small mock battle, from which the Filipinos would be excluded. The city would then be surrendered to the US forces only. The 'battle' took place on 13 August 1898, starting with a naval bombardment of one of Intramuros's forts. By noon the Spanish had surrendered and the fight was over.

## BRITISH OCCUPATION

Early in the 17th century the Spanish fought off several Dutch attempts to take Manila, but in the 18th century were unable to hold off the British. When the Seven Years' War broke out between Britain and France, Spain found itself allied on the French side by royal blood links. The British attacked and took Manila in 1762, though they were unable to extend control throughout the Philippines. When peace was restored in Europe, Britain handed Manila back to Spain, its troops pulling out in 1764.

## Ermita and Malate ★

These two districts, running southwards along the shore of Manila Bay, are well frequented by visitors. Here lie most of the hotels and many services that visitors need, such as travel agencies, money changers and souvenir shops. Although the main thoroughfare, **Roxas Boulevard**, is lined with high-rise buildings, some of them luxury hotels, much of the area is actually rather rundown, though things have improved in recent years.

At the southern end, the **Zoological and Botanical Garden** is a park that gives an introduction to the country's wildlife, although sadly most of the animals are not kept in good conditions. Open 07:00–18:00 daily.

Further south, on Roxas Boulevard, is the **Metropolitan Museum** (open 09:00–18:00 Mon–Sat), a modern building housing rotating exhibitions of foreign and Philippine art. Almost directly opposite, on land reclaimed from the bay, is the **Cultural Center of the Philippines**, which houses not only a large theatre where cultural performances are frequently shown, but also the **Museo ng Kalinangang Pilipino** (open 09:00–18:00 Tue–Sun), a beautiful museum housing an exhibition on different aspects of traditional Filipino costume, music and dance. It is well worth a visit.

**Left:** *A performance of traditional dancing at the Nayong Pilipino cultural village. Such performances are held every Sunday.*
**Opposite:** *Manila, seen from the Manila Hotel, looking along Roxas Boulevard and the shore of Manila Bay.*

To the east of Ermita, in the district of Paco, is **Paco Park**. This is a pleasant circular walled garden, an oasis in the middle of the city, shaded by some enormous trees.

### Nayong Pilipino ★★

Next to the airport's runways is this interesting cultural village-cum-park. Scattered in its grounds are numerous 'villages' – clusters of houses representing the architecture of different parts of the Philippines. One of the best is Ifugao Village, a cluster of thatched huts from the Cordillera Central of northern Luzon, complete with miniature rice terraces on which rice really is grown.

At one end of a lake are arranged several villages of the southern Philippines, mainly Mindanao and Sulu – groups of houses built in a pleasing architectural style. On Sundays the Mindanao village puts on dance performances. These villages are excellent places to pick up souvenirs of folk handicrafts, each one selling products representative of their part of the country. Close to the Sulu village is the **Museum of Ethnology**, which has an exhibition on the lives of the various ethnic groups of the Philippines.

In another part of the park is a walk-through aviary that contains a collection of Philippine birds. It is rather short on variety, but interesting nonetheless – the trees inside the aviary are so dense it can be quite difficult to see the birds! Open 06:00–21:00 daily.

## PEOPLE'S POWER

One of Asia's most famous modern uprisings took place in Manila in February 1986, following the rigging of presidential elections by then-president Ferdinand Marcos. Marcos claimed that he had defeated his opponent, Corazon Aquino, but when international observers reported the results fraudulent, thousands of people took to the streets. Defence minister **Juan Ponce Enrile** and deputy army chief **General Fidel Ramos** (who later became president) joined the opposition, along with a large section of the army. At separate ceremonies both Marcos and Aquino were sworn in as president. When forces loyal to Marcos moved down one of Manila's main arteries, **EDSA**, to attack the rebels at their base, their way was blocked by hundreds of thousands of people. Marcos was taken into exile by the US military, and ever since then the event has been marked on 25 February by parades along EDSA.

**Above:** *The massive entrance to the Stock Exchange Tower opens out onto Ayala Avenue.*

## MAKATI

Makati is the commercial hub of the capital, if not the entire country, and it's here that many banks and industrial or trading companies have their headquarters. Here you will also find some of the best shopping centres, restaurants and nightclubs, along with the country's smartest hotels.

While most visitors come to Makati for shopping and nightlife, there are also a few opportunities for sightseeing in the area. The first is the **Ayala Museum**, situated on Makati Avenue – an excellent museum that traces the Philippines' history from earliest settlement through to the EDSA Revolution of 1986. It makes use of 63 dioramas, extremely well-made models of events that capture critical moments in the country's history. Open 09:00–18:00 Tue–Fri, 10:00–19:00 Sat and Sun.

On the southeastern side of Makati is **Forbes Park**, an exclusive residential area for the wealthiest Filipinos. Nearby is a golf course, and to the south of that is the **American Cemetery and Memorial**, last resting place for many of the Americans that gave their lives for the Philippines.

## SHOPPING AND ENTERTAINMENT

For the visitor, shopping and entertainment opportunities are concentrated around Makati and the Ermita/Malate area. The latter has quite a large number of small bars and restaurants, mainly spread out along **Mabini** and **Adriatico** Streets. There are a number of souvenir and handicraft shops in this area. Handicrafts can also be bought in the main department stores, such as Rustans, Robinsons and SM, which, along with many other shops, are concentrated at **Harrison Plaza** (near the zoo) and **Robinsons Mall**, at the northern end of Adriatico Street.

In Makati, the choice of places to visit is huge. Most of the shopping is based around the **Ayala Center**, where you will find the enormous **Glorietta Mall** and also the **Landmark**. Close by is **Greenbelt Square**, where there is another mall, along with several restaurants and a cinema. As with Ermita/Malate, some of the best places to buy handicrafts are the department stores, particularly in the Landmark. The streets around Greenbelt and the Ayala Center are lined with a wide variety of restaurants.

Northeast of Makati is **Mandaluyong**, another commercial centre that rivals Makati. Here are several more shopping malls, including the **Shangri-La Plaza** and the enormous **Megamall**.

If you wish to attend cultural performances, these often take place at the **Cultural Center**. Alternatively, there are frequent free performances at the open-air theatre in **Rizal Park**. On Friday and Saturday evenings from January to June, Baluarte de San Diego in **Intramuros** is the venue for free dance performances by highly reputable dance troupes. Contact the Department of Tourism for details.

### EIGHT CITIES

Metro Manila comprises eight cities – Manila, Pasay, Makati, Caloocan, Quezon, Pasig, Mandaluyong and Muntinlupa – and is home to 12 million people, making it the largest metropolis in the Philippines.

**Below:** *A gun emplacement on Corregidor Island serves as a reminder of the grim battles fought here.*

## CORREGIDOR ISLAND

The fortress island of Corregidor lies a 2–3 hour ferry journey to the southwest. Initially fortified by the Spanish, Corregidor was quite heavily fought over by Spanish, American and Japanese invaders, who all recognized its key role in controlling Manila's shipping. Today, the island stands as a memorial to those times, with not only a Spanish lighthouse remaining, but also many of the heavy American fortifications and several memorials to the bloody events. Most visitors come on a day trip, but there is accommodation for those wishing to stay overnight. Ferries leave at 08:00 daily from the wharf close to the Cultural Center.

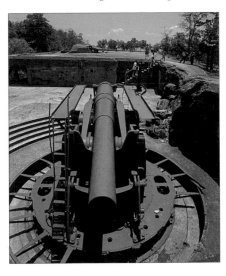

# Metro Manila at a Glance

BEST TIMES TO VISIT

Manila's rainy season lasts Jun–Oct, when parts of the city are often flooded and getting around can be difficult. The best time is **Dec–Mar**, when it is sunny, humidity is low and temperatures not too high. Apr–May can be very hot.

GETTING THERE

Ninoy Aquino International Airport is the Philippines' main international gateway, served by airlines from around the world. All major Asian airlines fly here. The national carrier, Philippine Airlines, also provides direct links with North America and Australia, though it has given up its European routes. Travellers from Europe will have to fly indirectly.

GETTING AROUND

Manila is highly congested and getting around can be slow. Allow plenty of time for journeys and do not try to do too much in one day. The **bus** system is a shambles, and **jeepneys**, though plentiful, are crowded, hot and uncomfortable. Air-conditioned minibuses called *tamaraws* are rather more comfortable. Manila's **taxis** are air conditioned, very inexpensive, metered only for distance and by far the best way to get around town. The crowded but convenient **Light Rail Transit** (LRT) runs north-south through the Chinatown-Ermita-Malate-Pasay areas, while the **Metro**

**Rail Transit** (MRT) loops along the EDSA Boulevard between Manila and much of Metro Manila, including the modern downtown areas of Makati and Mandaluyong.

WHERE TO STAY

*LUXURY*
**Makati Shangri-La Hotel**, Ayala Avenue, corner Makati Avenue, Makati City 1200, Metro Manila, tel: 02 813 8888, fax: 02 813 5499, e-mail: slm@shangri-la.com web: www.shangri-la.com Luxurious hotel in the centre of Makati, next to Ayala Center.
**EDSA Shangri-La Hotel**, 1 Garden Way, Ortigas Center, Mandaluyong City 1650, Metro Manila, tel: 02 633 8888, fax: 02 631 1067, e-mail: esl@shangri-la.com web: www.shangri-la.com Luxurious hotel with gardens, large pool, in the commercial hub of Mandaluyong.
**The Manila Hotel**, 1 Rizal Park, Manila 0913, tel: 02 527 0011, fax: 02 527 0022, e-mail: reservn@manila-hotel.com.ph web: www.manila-hotel.com.ph Opulent and refined. Superb views of Manila Bay.
**Galleria Manila**, One Asia Development Bank Avenue, Pasig, Manila, 1655, tel: 02 633 7111, e-mail: reservations @holiday-inn.galleria-mla.com web: www.holiday-inn.com Hotel in heart of Mandaluyong, Metro Manila's newest shopping/entertainment district.

**Hotel Sofitel Philippine Plaza Manila**, CCP Complex, Roxas Boulevard, Pasay, Metro Manila 1300, tel: 02 551 5555, fax: 02 551 5610, e-mail: room.reservations@ sofitelmanila.com web: www.sofitel.com

*MID-RANGE*
**Traders Hotel Manila**, 3001 Roxas Boulevard, Pasay City 1305, Metro Manila, tel: 02 523 7011, fax: 02 522 3985, e-mail: thm@shangri-la.com web: www.shangri-la.com Comfortable, well-run business hotel. Views of Manila Bay.
**Swagman Hotel Ermita Manila**, 411 A Flores St, Ermita, Manila, tel: 02 523 8541, fax: 02 522 3663, e-mail: bookings@ swaggy.com web: www. swaggy.com The Philippine headquarters of the Swagman chain offering value-for-money hotels and travel services over much of the country.
**Las Palmas Hotel**, 1616 A Mabini St, Malate, Manila, tel: 02 521 1000, fax: 02 523 6917, e-mail: sales@ laspalmashotel.com.ph web: www.laspalmashotel.com.ph Modern hotel in Ermita/Malate.
**Lotus Garden Hotel**, 1227 A Mabini, cnr P Faura St, Manila, tel: 02 522 1515, fax: 02 522 0768, e-mail: lotus@ citygardenhotels.com web: www.citygardenhotels.com Value-for-money hotel in the centre of the Ermita/Malate area. Rooms facing the street can be noisy; get one at the back.

## Metro Manila at a Glance

**Rothman Hotel**, 1633 M Adriatico St, Malate, Manila, tel: 02 523 4501, e-mail: info@rothmanhotel.com web: www.rothmanhotel.com
**City Garden Hotel Makati**, 7870 Makati Ave, cnr Kalayaan Ave, Makati, Metro Manila, tel: 02 899 1111, e-mail: makatireserve@citygardenhotels.com web: www.citygardenhotels.com

### BUDGET
**Robelle Mansion**, 877 JP Rizal St, Makati, Metro Manila, tel: 02 899 7388, fax: 02 899 7390, e-mail: robelle@i-manila.com.ph web: www.divephil.com/rmansion In the style of a Spanish villa, surrounded by palm trees; an oasis in the city.
**Oasis Park Hotel**, 1032–4 Belen St, Paco, Manila, tel: 02 521 2371–5, e-mail: info@oasispark.com web: www.oasispark.com Good value, close to but at a quiet distance from the hubbub of Ermita.

### WHERE TO EAT
**Sala**, 610 J Nakpil St, Malate, Manila, tel: 02 524 6770, e-mail: sala@pacific.net.ph Small, selling Western food.
**Zen Restaurant**, Glorietta III, Level 1, Ayala Center, Makati City, Metro Manila, tel: 02 892 6851. Popular; Japanese.
**Café Adriatico**, 1790 M Adriatico St, Malate, Manila, tel: 02 523 7924. Long-established café; snacks during the day, evening meals.
**Café Havana**, cnr M Adriatico & Remedios St, Malate, Manila, tel: 02 521 8097. Popular Cuban restaurant; loud music.
**Via Mare Oyster Bar**, Greenbelt 3, Paseo de Roxas, Makati City, Metro Manila, tel: 02 815 1918, e-mail: info@viamare.com.ph Seafood restaurant in the heart of Manila's modern district.
**Queen's Crystal Garden Restaurant**, 146B Jupiter St, Makati, Metro Manila 1209, tel: 02 895 1316, e-mail: queens_rest@hotmail.com web: www.queenstandoor.com Indian and Indonesian cuisine.

### TOURS AND EXCURSIONS
For the trip to Corregidor Island contact **Sun Cruises**. For other trips contact **Swagman Travel**. Some car-hire companies offer self-drive and chauffeur-driven hire cars. To arrange diving trips before leaving Manila try **Dive Buddies Philippines**, for complete diving packages.

### USEFUL CONTACTS
**Department of Tourism**, Dept of Tourism Bldg, TM Kalaw St, Ermita, Manila, tel: 02 524 2345 or 525 6114, airport office: 02 832 2964, e-mail: ncr@tourism.gov.ph
web: www.tourism.gov.ph or www.wowphilippines.com.ph
**Philippine Airlines**, Makati ticket office, 2/F Power Realty Building, 1012 A Arnaiz Rd, Makati 1223, Metro Manila, tel: 02 892 7339, reservations tel: 02 855 8888, e-mail: online booking@pal.com.ph web: www.philippinesairlines.com
**Swagman Travel**, 411 A Flores St, Ermita, Manila, tel: 02 523 8541, fax: 02 522 3663, e-mail: bookings@swaggy.com
**Safari Rent-a-Car**, 1839 Eureka St, La Paz Village, Makati City, Metro Manila, tel: 02 890 3606, e-mail: info@safarirentacarinc.com web: www.safarirentacarinc.com
**Rentacar Nissan**, Manila Peninsula Hotel, Ayala cnr Makati Ave, Makati, Metro Manila, tel: 02 854 7099, e-mail: nissanreservation@nissanrentacar.com web: www.nissanrentacar.com
**Dive Buddies Philippines**, G/F Robelle Mansion Building, 877 JP Rizal St, Makati, Metro Manila, tel: 02 899 7388, fax: 02 899 7393, e-mail: center@divephil.com web: www.divephil.com
**Police**: Emergency: 117; Non-emergency: 02 723 0401.

| MANILA | J | F | M | A | M | J | J | A | S | O | N | D |
|---|---|---|---|---|---|---|---|---|---|---|---|---|
| AVERAGE TEMP. °F | 79 | 81 | 82 | 84 | 86 | 84 | 82 | 82 | 82 | 82 | 81 | 81 |
| AVERAGE TEMP. °C | 26 | 27 | 28 | 29 | 30 | 29 | 28 | 28 | 28 | 28 | 27 | 27 |
| RAINFALL in | 0.6 | 0.2 | 0.4 | 0.7 | 5.7 | 11.2 | 16 | 18.3 | 13.9 | 8.8 | 4.8 | 2 |
| RAINFALL mm | 16 | 6 | 9 | 17 | 146 | 284 | 408 | 464 | 352 | 224 | 122 | 52 |
| DAYS OF RAINFALL | 4 | 2 | 2 | 3 | 9 | 17 | 22 | 22 | 20 | 17 | 11 | 7 |

# 3
# Northern Luzon and Batanes Islands

Encompassing the main body of Luzon, the largest of the Philippines' islands, this area covers all the land north of Manila. Much of the landscape here is quite different from the customary Philippine image of sun-drenched beaches and glorious coral reefs. There are beaches to visit in and around **Subic Bay** and **San Fernando**, but the region's main interest lies inland. Home to tribal minorities, the area's high, rugged mountains and pine forests offer a rare opportunity to escape the tropical heat. The city of **Baguio** is the capital of this region, beyond which the rough **Halsema Road** links up many of the mountain areas, including the beautiful village of **Sagada** and the mighty rice terraces of **Banaue**. At the southern edge of the mountains stands Mount Pinatubo, whose 1991 eruption was one of the world's biggest in the whole of the 20th century. Nearby, the **rainforests** and relatively tame wildlife of Subic Bay offer a rare opportunity for visitors to experience this type of environment.

On the northwest coast of Luzon is the town of **Vigan**, one of the oldest Spanish settlements in the country and the best preserved of all. Here, an entire section of the town consists of streets lined with Castilian houses, and it is possible to stay in several old Spanish villas.

The most northerly point of the Philippines lies in the **Batanes Islands**, closer to Taiwan than to mainland Luzon. Wild, remote and storm-battered, the landscape and high cliffs of these islands have been compared with those of Ireland.

## DON'T MISS

\*\*\* **Subic Forest:** accessible tropical lowland rainforest, with reasonably tame wildlife.
\*\*\* **Sagada:** a village high in the mountains, with walking trails and caves to explore.
\*\* **Rice terraces of Banaue:** 2000-year-old rice terraces high on the mountain slopes.
\*\* **Hundred Islands:** a group of small islands surrounded by clear, shallow sea.
\*\* **Batanes Islands:** wild, remote islands with dramatic scenery.
\* **Vigan:** the best preserved of all the old Spanish towns in the Philippines.

**Opposite:** *Rice terraces carved into the Cordillera Central mountains.*

## BATAAN AND ZAMBALES

The Bataan Peninsula forms the western wall of Manila Bay, protecting the capital from the westerly winds of the South China Sea. To the north lies Zambales province, composed mostly of the Zambales Mountains and a narrow coastal plain. The most important development in the area is **Subic Bay**, along with the adjacent town of **Olongapo**.

*Above: The Subic Yacht Club is a powerful symbol of the Subic Bay Freeport's growing importance in the leisure and tourism business.*

### CLIMATE

The west coast is rainy from June to October or November, and then dry and sunny from November to May. In the mountains it is similar, though on the eastern side rain also comes in February–March. The Batanes Islands are stormy and wet for much of the year, being dry only from March to May. Almost all areas are dry **March–May**, though these are also the hottest months. Up in the Cordillera Central, even daytime temperatures are pleasantly cool. People from hot climates may find the night-time temperatures here a bit cold during January and February.

### Subic Bay **

About 130km (80 miles) from Manila, the southeastern chunk of this large enclosed bay was an American naval base until the US military pulled out of the Philippines in 1992. It was originally developed as a naval port by the Spanish, but was taken over by the Americans in 1899 during the Spanish–American War. It was occupied by the Japanese during World War II, but returned to American control in 1945. During the Vietnam War it became the USA's largest overseas military base.

When the Americans pulled out, economic disaster loomed for the local people, but instead the site was turned into a freeport and economic zone, a move which has been remarkably successful. Today, the urban part of **Subic Bay Freeport** (SBF) is a modern town. Because of the port's duty-free status, entry and exit are controlled: upon arrival you will need to do some form filling, and when you leave you may be searched.

For the general visitor, the main attractions include an 18-hole **golf course**, three **beaches** and the **forest**. For water-sports enthusiasts, this is a great place for **windsurfing**, especially during the southwest monsoon (June–October), and is one of the Philippines' two major **wreck diving** locations. The bay is strewn with wrecks and it is possible to dive onto several old warships.

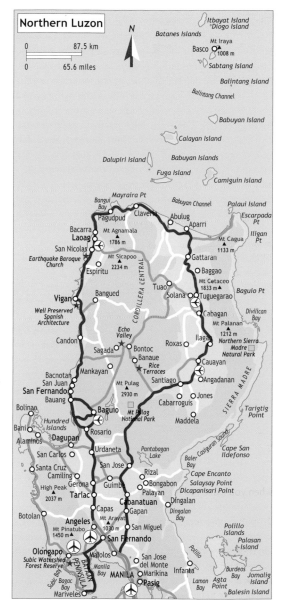

**Northern Luzon**

0   87.5 km
0   65.6 miles

N

Itbayat Island
Diogo Island
Batanes Islands
Basco   Mt Iraya
1008 m
Sabtang Island
Balintang Island
Balintang Channel
Babuyan Island
Calayan Island
Dalupiri Island
Babuyan Islands
Fuga Island
Camiguin Island
Mayraira Pt
Bangui Bay
Babuyan Channel
Palaui Island
Escarpada Pt
Pagudpud   Claveria   Abulug
Aparri
Bacarra   Mt Agnamala
Laoag
San Nicolas   1786 m
Earthquake Baroque
Church   Espiritu   Mt Sicapoo
2234 m
Iligan Pt
Mt Cagua
1133 m
Gattaran
Baggao
Vigan   Bangued
Tuao
Mt Cetaceo
1833 m
Baguio Pt
Well Preserved
Spanish
Architecture
Solana   Tuguegarao
Cabagan   Divilican Bay
Candon   Echo Valley
Mt Palanan
1212 m
Northern Sierra Madre Natural Park
Sagada   Bontoc   Roxas   Ilagan
Banaue
Rice Terraces
Cauayan
Bacnotan   Mankayan
San Juan
San Fernando
Bauang
Santiago
Angadanan
Mt Pulag
2930 m
Cabarroguis   Jones
Bolinao
Baguio   Mt Pulag National Park
Maddela
Tarigtig
Point
Bani   Hundred Islands
Rosario
Alaminos   Dagupan
Urdaneta
Pantabangan Lake
Cape San Ildefonso
San Carlos
San Jose
Baler Bay
Santa Cruz   Camiling
Rizal
Cape Encanto
High Peak
2037 m   Gerona   Guimba
Bongabon
Salaysay Point
Dicapanisari Point
Tarlac
Palayan
Capas   Cabanatuan
Dingalan
Botolan   Gapan
Dingalan Bay
Angeles   Mt Arayat
1030 m   San Miguel
Mt Pinatubo
1450 m   San Fernando
Polillo
Islands
Palasan Island
Olongapo   Malolos
San Jose del Monte
Subic Watershed
Forest Reserve
Manila Bay
Marikina   Infanta
Burdeos Bay   Jomalig Island
Subic   Bagac
Bay   Bay
MANILA
Pasig
Lamon Bay   Agta Point   Balesin Island
Mariveles

CORDILLERA CENTRAL

SIERRA MADRE

BATAAN PENINSULA

Polillo

Casiguran Sound

## SUNKEN WRECKS

As a naval base set up at the end of the 19th century, Subic Bay has seen plenty of action. Numerous wrecks litter the floor of the bay, and several are now used for wreck diving. The oldest of these is the *San Quintin*, sunk by the Spanish in 1898 in an attempt to block part of the bay's entrance and prevent an American attack. All the other wrecks date from World War II, the biggest being the ex-*USS New York*, a large battleship that was scuppered by the Americans in 1941. Other wrecks include the *Oryoku Maru*, a Japanese cruise liner sunk by US aircraft in 1944, and the *Seian Maru*, a Japanese freighter sunk in 1945.

**Below:** *A member of Subic's Jungle Environmental Survival Training Center shows how to make fire without matches.*

## Subic Watershed Forest ★★★

The 10,000ha (25,000-acre) forest surrounding Subic Bay is one of the last remaining areas of tropical lowland rainforest in Luzon and, together with forest outside the SBF, makes up Subic–Bataan Natural Park, one of the country's highest priority protected areas. Roads crisscross the forest, making access easy, and with almost no hunting for the past 100 years the wildlife has become quite tame. Macaques are a common sight, and there are also forest birds, many of them unique to the Philippines. A big attraction is a colony of fruit bats that roost during the daytime in tall trees near the district of Cubi.

Many parts of the forest have been increasingly developed for tourism, and there are now a number of attractions. These include **JEST**, the Jungle Environmental Survival Training Camp, where **Aeta** tribesmen can give training in jungle survival skills. Not far away is **Pamu-laklakin**, a model Aeta village, where locals put on cultural shows. Remoter areas, such as in the Ilanin Forest, are **Zoobic Safari**, a zoo most noted for its drive-through tiger section, and **Treetop Adventure**, a park with walkways and zip wires in the forest canopy. Hiking in the forest is also possible, particularly at **Triboa Bay Mangrove Park**, where coastal forest and mangroves can be explored. Another coastal site is home to **Subic Bay Ocean Adventure**, a marine aquarium that puts on regular shows with dolphins, killer whales and sea lions.

**Opposite:** *A resort and beach near Barrio Barretto in Subic Bay.*
**Right:** *Light aircraft for hire at Clark Field, with Mount Pinatubo in the distance.*

## Olongapo *

Situated immediately outside the main gates to Subic Bay, the town of Olongapo has always provided labour for the base and, in turn, the SBF. Apart from a number of restaurants and bars, the town itself has very little of interest, although it does make rather a good base from which to explore the rest of the Subic Bay area as its hotels are considerably cheaper than those inside the SBF. North of Olongapo, further into the bay but outside the SBF, are a number of very attractive sandy beaches, particularly those at the village of **Barrio Barretto**.

## Angeles and Mount Pinatubo *

Approximately 80km (50 miles) to the northeast of Olongapo is Angeles, which until 1992 was the site of **Clark Airforce Base**, another major centre for the US military. Situated right at the foot of Mount Pinatubo, both the military base and the town were devastated by the volcano's 1991 eruption. Since the American withdrawal **Clark Field** (as it is nowadays called), following Subic's example, became a duty-free economic zone, encouraging industries to move in and touting its potential as a major new international airport. In the town outside Clark Field, business is booming as before, and the bars and brothels that once catered to the American GIs are now attracting those tourists who travel up here from Manila specifically for the nightlife.

Thankfully, Angeles does have another role. It is the starting point for treks into Pinatubo's lahar fields, sometimes going as far as the crater rim. In Clark Field you can also hire an airplane for sightseeing tours around Pinatubo. Such flights must be undertaken early in the morning before thermal currents build up.

---

**SUBIC WATERSHED FOREST**

This tropical lowland rainforest is one of the few remaining areas of its type in Luzon. Protected by the American military when this was a naval base, it is now a vitally important nature reserve. The forest was partly damaged by Mount Pinatubo's eruption, but today the only reminders of that are the unusually large numbers of dead trees. Some of the best forest is in the old Naval Magazine area (now called Subic Bay Nature Park), and here the forest comes right down to the shoreline, to include some rare beach forest which merges with mangroves.

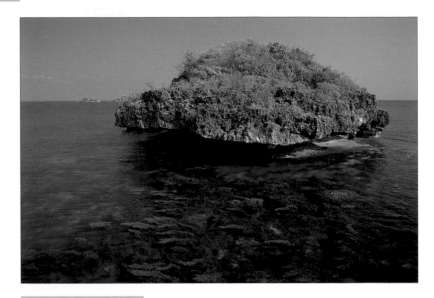

## THE MOUNT PINATUBO ERUPTION

Pinatubo lay dormant for 450 years, but in March 1991 it began to rumble. It erupted on 9 June, and on 15 June there followed a massive explosion that shot rocks and ash 30,000m (98,400ft) into the sky and took 300m (980ft) off the volcano's height. Day was turned into night even as far away as Manila, 90km (55 miles) to the southeast, and whole communities were buried under ash. As the volcano calmed down, so a typhoon whipped through the region, the heavy rain sending torrents of **lahar** down the slopes and sweeping across the lowlands. Whole towns were destroyed and nearly 700 people killed. Today, lahar rivers remain a major threat during each rainy season.

## CENTRAL WEST COAST

About 90km (55 miles) north of Angeles you come to the coast of the **Lingayen Gulf**. Around here are a number of locations worth visiting. To the west are the **Hundred Islands**, while to the east lie the beautiful beaches of the **San Fernando** area.

### Hundred Islands ★★

A scattering of limestone islands in a shallow azure sea, this area has been designated a National Recreation Area. The nearest large town is **Alaminos**, reachable from Olongapo/Subic via the picturesque Zambales coast road. From Angeles or Manila you would follow the congested main highway. Alaminos is a chaotic town, but fortunately there is no need to stay there. Instead, continue on another 5km (3 miles) to the coastal village of **Lucap**, where boats can be hired for a tour of the islands. The shoreline at Lucap is not pretty either, with its scrappy hotel development and half filled-in fish ponds. Boats to tour the Hundred Islands can be hired either from the jetty or one of the waterside hotels.

Most of the islands are tiny and impossible to land on, but a few have beaches where boats can come ashore. **Governor's Island** is the first of these. Here a footpath climbs to the summit of a hill, from which there is a good view of the little archipelago. Further out is **Children's Island**, quite a large place with more footpaths and views. There are cottages to let here; there is no electricity and you have to bring all your own food and water, but a kerosene lamp is provided. One of the outermost islands is **Quezon Island**, which because of its beautiful sandy beach attracts the most visitors.

### San Fernando (La Union) ★

Not to be confused with the inland town of San Fernando just north of Manila and in Pampanga province, this coastal town is known for its beaches that stretch along the coast north and south. Most beach life is concentrated around the village of **Bauang**, approximately 10km (6 miles) south. Here a string of well-developed beach resorts cater to people coming up from Manila at the weekends. Though it is a pleasant spot, the sand is rather grey and the beach is so crowded with boats (mostly there for tourism, not fishing) that at high tide it is often necessary to walk in the water!

Just a few kilometres north of San Fernando, at the village of **San Juan**, things are completely different. The sand is still rather grey here, but the beach is huge, both wide and several kilometres long, and pounded by surf. At the southern end of the beach, where the surf is at its best, are several surf camps. Development along the beach has been light, and the handful of resorts are still well separated from each other.

**BEST BUYS**

Some of the Philippines' best handicrafts come from the Cordillera Central, where woodcarving, weaving and silversmithing have been integral parts of life for many generations. Carved figures of pre-Christian deities are common, silver jewellery is attractive and unique in style, while woven fabrics, either as clothing or decorative wall hangings, are widely available. Good places to buy products include Mines View Park and the Easter School of Weaving in Baguio, and a wide variety of small shops in Banaue.

**Opposite:** *A rocky islet, one of the many that make up Hundred Islands.* **Below:** *Boats fill the beach at Bauang, the main beach resort in northern Luzon.*

## THE FOUNDING OF VIGAN

When the Spanish arrived in the 16th century, Vigan had already been an important trading port for several centuries. **Juan de Salcedo**, grandson of Legaspi, arrived in 1572 and set up a Spanish base here, which he called Villa Fernandina. The area became his *encomienda* and the town became the Spanish capital of the far north. Salcedo did not live to see the town develop, however. He died in 1576, aged 27.

**Below:** *Crisologo St is lined with Spanish houses that recall the colonial past.*

## THE NORTHWEST

The northwest is a very pleasant rural area, the journey northwards from San Fernando passing through an agricultural landscape rich in rice, maize and tobacco. This was the homeland of the dictator **Ferdinand Marcos**, and he is still something of a hero in these parts. The first, and most interesting, town in the area is **Vigan**, an old Spanish town.

## Vigan ★★

Situated 139km (90 miles) north of San Fernando and 400km (250 miles) from Manila, Vigan was an important port long before the Spanish arrived in 1572. Today it is known as the fourth-oldest Spanish settlement in the country and without doubt the best preserved. One entire section of the city consists of nothing but cobbled streets lined with ancient Spanish houses. One street in particular, **Crisologo Street**, is of importance as it is lined with furniture workshops – as well as one place that still weaves with a traditional hand loom. Motorized vehicles are not allowed in this area, the only transport being horse-drawn carriages, or *calesa*.

At the northern end of the old town is the beautiful **St Paul's Cathedral**, with next door the **Archbishop's Palace**. Nearby is the **Ayala Museum** which traces much of Vigan's history (open 08:30–11:30 and 13:30–16:30 Mon–Fri). The museum is housed in the birthplace

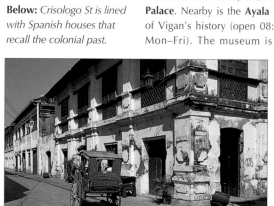

of José Burgos, an early Filipino patriot executed in 1872 by the Spanish. At the southwestern end of town are several **pottery workshops**, where it is possible to watch large *burnay* pots being made, traditionally used for the storage of foodstuffs. In the centre of the old town there are a number of old villas that can be visited, of which the most beautiful is **Villa Angela**. Here, the elegant furnishings are a pleasing blend of Spanish, Chinese and Malay. Villa Angela also doubles up as a hotel; one of the management's proud boasts is that Tom Cruise once stayed here!

Beyond Vigan the coast road continues through the city of **Laoag**, passing along the way the **Paoay Church** and also Marcos's birthplace at **Batac**. Further north, there are some remote beaches at **Pagudpud**, shortly before **Mayraira Point**, the most northerly point of mainland Luzon.

## CORDILLERA CENTRAL

This mountainous region is the very heart of northern Luzon, to which many visitors flock, if only to get away from the lowland heat! The people here, many of them from tribal minorities, are proud and independent, having for many years successfully resisted control by the Spanish and Americans. Today, with their stupendous scenery and unique culture, the mountains offer a view of the Philippines that is radically diferent from the usual one of sand and surf.

### Baguio **

Most visitors to the Philippines begin their tour of the mountains in Baguio, the capital of Benguet province and by far the largest settlement in the Cordillera. At an altitude of some 1500m (4900ft) the air is pleasantly cool, though in the downtown area it is hard to find much truth in the tourist literature's claims for Baguio's relaxing atmosphere, views and scented pine trees. Actually, the city centre is just as congested and polluted as any other city in the Philippines.

**Above:** *A view of the Cordillera Central mountains seen near Baguio, with Mount Pulag (2930m), highest mountain on Luzon, in the distance.*

### DIEGO AND GABRIELA SILANG

Diego Silang led a rebellion in the Vigan area in December 1762, inspired by an announcement by the British (who had just taken over Manila) that the natives should be left to run their own lives. However, the Spanish bishop of Vigan, Bernardo Ustariz, hired an assasin, Miguel Vicos, who killed Diego in May 1763. The remaining rebels, led by Diego's wife Gabriela Silang, continued the rebellion but were eventually caught and executed. Gabriela Silang was the last to die – she was hanged in Vigan on 20 September 1763.

**Above:** *The Cordillera's vegetable farms, such as this one on the slopes of Mt Pulag, supply most of the Philippines' temperate fruit and vegetables, from strawberries to cabbages, carrots and potatoes.*

## MOUNT PULAG

Northeast of Baguio stands Mount Pulag, at 2930m (9610ft) the highest mountain in Luzon, and often wrongly claimed to be the second highest in the Philippines. A national park, the mountain's highest areas are covered with grass and dwarf bamboo less than a 1m (3ft) high, while a little lower is a large area of dense mossy forest, characterized by short, gnarled trees draped in moss and lichen. Below the mossy forest is a forest of Benguet pines, though this has been badly damaged by encroaching vegetable farms.

That does not mean that the downtown area is not enjoyable. **Session Road**, the main street, is a colourful and lively place with a range of shops and restaurants, while at the bottom of the hill the **city market** is one of the most interesting in the country. Nearby, **Burnham Park** with its boating lake is a welcome city centre oasis.

To enjoy the feeling of being in a mountain resort it is important to stay in one of the hotels on the eastern side of the city, where parks and pine forests merge with the housing. Here, the **Botanical Garden** and **Wright Park** are pleasant forested places, while further out is **Mines View Park**, a lookout point with a spectacular view across the mountains. This is also a good place to pick up some **mountain handicrafts**, as there are many stalls selling an array of weaving and woodcarving products.

Most impressive is **Club John Hay**, a huge rambling park containing a golf course and country club, tennis courts, restaurants, a hotel and attractive woodlands. Originally called Camp John Hay, this was another centre for the US military, this time a recreation facility.

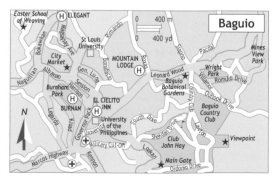

Places of interest to the north and northwest of the city include the **St Louis University Silver Shop**, where visitors can watch silversmiths at work, and the **Easter School of Weaving**, where the same applies for people working on traditional hand looms. The end products can be bought at both these places.

### The Halsema Road **

Linking Baguio with the town of **Bontoc**, the capital of Mountain province and about 130km (95 miles) to the north, this is the most spectacular road in the Philippines, offering superb views of the Cordillera mountains, including Mount Pulag (2930m; 9610ft), the tallest mountain on Luzon. The highest point reached by the road itself is on a pass at 2255m (7396ft) – the highest point on any road in the country – which is about a third of the way towards Bontoc. Unfortunately, the Halsema does not offer a gentle ride, since most of it is unpaved and in very bad condition. Even in the dry season the journey takes seven hours, and in the rains it may be completely impassable.

### Sagada ***

A left turn off the Halsema Road just a few kilometres before Bontoc leads high up into the mountains to one of the Cordillera's gems: the village of Sagada, nestling in forest at an altitude of 1400m (4600ft). With its cool air and relaxed atmosphere, this is a genuine mountain retreat. Hiking trails head off to a number of mountain peaks, waterfalls and caves. The last of these are especially interesting since the people here have traditionally buried their dead in caves or in hanging coffins attached to the sides of cliffs. It is still quite a common practice today.

> **MOUNTAIN TRIBES**
>
> The best-known tribes of the Cordillera Central are the **Ifugao**, **Bontoc** and **Kalinga**, though there are a number of other groups, such as the **Ibaloi** and **Kalanguya**, both of which live on the slopes of Mount Pulag. These farming peoples (it was the Ifugao who built the rice terraces around Banaue about 2000 years ago) were also all quite warlike in the past, staging ritual attacks on their neighbours and regularly **head-hunting**. There have been a few reports that heads are still taken very occasionally, and it is known that the remotest villages in the Sierra Madre mountains, along the east coast of northern Luzon, still engage in ritual war.

**Below:** *Hanging coffins attached to a cliff in Echo Valley, Sagada.*

### A Life Apart

The people of the Batanes Islands have long lived an isolated life. About 230km (143 miles) from the Luzon mainland, 650km (406 miles) from Manila and 250km (160 miles) from Taiwan, the people here live completely surrounded by deep oceans. Until regular flights started a few years ago, the islanders were reliant on an infrequent freighter for essential supplies and the export of their main products – beef and goat's meat. Life continues to be simple, but was greatly modernized with the arrival in the 1990s of electricity, motor transport and television.

**Opposite:** *A view along the coast of Batan Island towards Mt Iraya (1008m).* **Below:** *A tiny farming village forms a tight cluster of houses in the Cordillera mountains near Banaue.*

Unfortunately, vandalism has forced the locals to close some of the caves, but one of the most interesting areas to explore, quite close to the village, is **Echo Valley**. This narrow gorge contains a number of caves as well as a cliff to which are attached several coffins. Although only one of the caves contains coffins, another is unusual for having an **underground river** flowing out of its mouth.

There are many caves more remote than these, but to explore them you need to hire a guide. This can be arranged at the tourist desk in Sagada's municipal office.

### Banaue and the Rice Terraces ★★

About 340km (200 miles) north of Manila and 150km (95 miles) from Baguio, the 2000-year-old rice terraces that cover the mountainsides around Banaue are touted as one of the must-see places of northern Luzon. With more than a little hyperbole they have been called the Eighth Wonder of the World, but even if they are not as spectacular as the tourist brochures would have the world believe, they are nevertheless beautiful and quite remarkable. The terraces immediately above the town of Banaue and visible from the **Banaue View Point** are the most accessible, but are less stunning than those around **Batad**, a village about 15km (10 miles) to the east by road and then needing a two-hour hike to reach.

## THE IVATAN

The Ivatan, the ethnic group that makes up almost the whole of the Batanes Islands' 14,000 population, are believed to be of pure Austronesian descent, their isolation precluding any overlay of more recent Malay or even Chinese immigration. Their language, as well as their way of life, is unique in the Philippines. A shy, yet friendly people, most of their economic activity revolves around pastoral farming, mainly the rearing of goats and cattle. Fishing is limited to close inshore work due to the rough seas. Locally built boats are sturdy monohulls, quite similar to the general shape of a Chinese junk.

## BATANES ISLANDS

This remote cluster of 10 islands represents the most northerly point of the Philippines, lying between the Luzon mainland and Taiwan, 650km (390 miles) north of Manila. Right in the path of virtually every typhoon that comes along, the islands are storm-battered and for much of the year barely accessible.

Three of the islands, **Batan**, **Itbayat** and **Sabtang**, are inhabited, the total population being about 14,000. Most of the people belong to the **Ivatan** ethnic group, with their own language and customs quite distinct from the mainland. Architecture is unique too, with thick stone walls and heavy thatching adapted to the harsh climate. The main town is **Basco**, on Batan, lying at the foot of 1008m (3306ft) Mount Iraya, an active volcano. Basco is a lovely little town with almost no traffic and very friendly people. Apart from Mount Iraya, much of the landscape consists of rolling hills on which cattle and goats graze, while the coast is a mixture of sheer cliffs and gentle bays with rocky islets offshore. Sabtang is similar, though the lifestyle here is more traditional than on Batan. Itbayat, though the largest island, is thinly populated and very difficult to reach.

These islands are for lovers of the remote and the outdoors. A number of hiking trails crisscross Batan, including one up Mount Iraya. You will need a guide on some of the more remote trails.

## TRADITIONAL CLOTHING

The Ivatans have some traditional clothing for use as rain gear, which is still produced and used locally. These are essentially raincapes, called *canaye* for men and *soot* for women, made from the fibres of the leaves off a small common palm, *Phoenix hansiana*. The particular variety used is unique to the Batanes Islands, but is closely related to a palm that is common in Taiwan and along the south China coast. They are still produced by hand in a few villages on Sabtang Island.

## Northern Luzon and Batanes Islands at a Glance

### BEST TIMES TO VISIT

For lowland areas in northern Luzon, weather patterns are the same as for Manila: rain Jun–Oct, dry Dec–May. Apr and May are the hottest months. In the mountains the rains last from Apr/May to Nov.

### GETTING THERE

Regular **flights** from Manila to Baguio, Subic, Angeles, Laoag and Basco. Buses from Manila to Angeles, San Fernando, Olongapo, Alaminos, Vigan, Laoag, Baguio and Banaue.

### GETTING AROUND

Frequent **bus** services go from Olongapo to Alaminos, and from Angeles to Alaminos. Take a **jeepney** or **tricycle** to Lucap. Buses run from Alaminos to San Fernando; you may have to change in Dagupan en route. From San Fernando, there are buses to Vigan, Laoag and Baguio. From Baguio to Sagada, take a bus to Bontoc and then backtrack by jeepney to Sagada. To go to Banaue, travel to Bontoc, and then take a bus to Banaue. Self-drive **cars** hired in Manila can be driven over this route, but be prepared for punctures. Set off with a full tank; filling stations are scarce.

### WHERE TO STAY

**Subic Bay**
*LUXURY*
**Subic Legenda Hotel**, 294 Waterfront Rd, Subic Bay Freeport Zone, Subic, Olangapo City, Zambales, tel: 047

232 9315, e-mail: sales@legendasubic.com web: www.legendasubic.com Modern hotel in commercial district.
**Subic International Hotel**, Rizal cnr St Rita Rds, Subic Bay Freeport Zone, Olangapo City 2200, Zambales, tel: 047 252 2222, fax: 047 894 5579, e-mail: sales@subichotel.com web: www.subichotel.com

**Olongapo**
*MID-RANGE*
**By the Sea Resort**, 99 National Highway, Barrio Baretto, Olongapo City, tel: 047 222 2888, e-mail: inquiry@bythesea.com.ph web: www.bythesea.com.ph North of the city.

**Angeles**
*MID-RANGE*
**Swagman Resort Hotel**, SL Orosa St, Diamond Subdivision, Angeles City 2009, Pampanga, tel: 045 322 5133, e-mail: bookings@angelescity.info web: www.swaggy.com

**Hundred Islands**
*MID-RANGE*
**Vista Delas Islas**, Lucap, Alaminos, Pangasinan, tel: 075 551 4455.

**San Fernando (La Union)**
*LUXURY*
**Cabana Beach Resort**, Paringao Bauang, La Union, tel: 072 607 6608, e-mail: cabana@pldtdsl.net web: www.cabana.com.ph
**Puerto de San Juan Beach Resort**, Ili Sur, San Juan,

La Union, tel/fax: 072 607 4328, e-mail: psj@puertodesanjuan.com web: www.puertodesanjuan.com

*MID-RANGE*
**Coconut Grove Beach Resort**, Paringao Bauang, La Union, tel: 072 607 6604, e-mail: resort@coco.com.ph web: www.coco.com.ph Just south of San Fernando.

**Vigan**
*MID-RANGE*
**El Juliana Hotel**, 5 Liberation Blvd, corner Quirino Ave, Vigan, Ilocos Sur, tel: 077 722 2994. Hotel in the old town; pool and restaurant.

*BUDGET*
**Villa Angela**, 26 Quirino Blvd, Vigan, Ilocos Sur, tel: 077 722 2914, e-mail: info@villangela.com web: www.villangela.com A beautiful Spanish-era mansion in the old town.

**Baguio**
*MID-RANGE*
**Burnham Hotel**, 20 Calderon St, Baguio, Benguet, tel: 074 442 2331, e-mail: burnhamhotel@gmail.com web: www.burnhamhotelbaguio.com
**El Cielito Inn Baguio**, 50 North Drive, Baguio, Benguet, tel: 074 443 4846, e-mail: stay@elcielitoinn.com web: www.elcielito-baguio.com

*BUDGET*
**Elegant Hotel and Restaurant**, 421 Magsaysay Ave, Baguio City, tel: 074 442 9322.

## Northern Luzon and Batanes Islands at a Glance

**Mountain Lodge**, 27 Leonard Wood Rd, Baguio City, Benguet, tel: 074 442 4544, e-mail: info@mountainlodge baguio.com web: www.moun tainlodgebaguio.com Old hotel, near Botanical Garden.

### Sagada
*MID-RANGE*
**George Guesthouse**, Dao-Angan, Sagada, Mountain Province, tel (cell): 0918 548 0406, e-mail: george.guest house@yahoo.com web: http://sagada.georgeinn. bravehost.com

*BUDGET*
**Residential Lodge**, Dagdag, Sagada, Mountain Province, tel (cell): 0919 672 8744, e-mail: eldone21@yahoo.com web: www.visitsagada.com/accom modation-residential-lodge/

### Banaue
*MID-RANGE*
**Banaue Hotel and Youth Hostel**, Iloque, Tam-an, Banaue, Ifugao, tel: 074 386 4087, web: www.philtourism.com/bhyh_de sc.html Banaue's largest hotel.

*BUDGET*
**Fairview Inn**, Banaue, Ifugao, tel: 074 386 4002. A pleasant and large house.
**People's Lodge Inn**, Poblacion, Banaue, tel: 074 386 4037. Guesthouse with restaurant.

### Basco
*BUDGET*
**Shanedel's Inn and Café**, Basco, Batanes.

**Ivatan Lodge**, Basco, Batanes. Accommodation is limited in the Batanes Islands, and there are few telephones to aid advance booking. Meals are usually eaten at the lodge.

### WHERE TO EAT

### Subic Bay
**New Feng Huang**, Subic Bay Venezia Hotel, 675 Canal Rd, Subic Bay Freeport, tel: 047 252 1888. Chinese food.
**Aresi**, Courtyard Inn, Waterfront Rd, Subic Bay Freeport, tel: 047 252 2367. Italian seafood restaurant.

### Baguio
**Café by the Ruins**, 23 Chuntug Rd, Baguio City, Benguet, tel: 074 442 4010. Popular vegetarian restaurant, rustic decor.
**Sizzling Plate**, 116 Session Rd, Baguio City, Benguet, tel: 074 442 4219. Steak house.

### SHOPPING

Duty-free shopping is available to foreign visitors in Subic Bay Freeport, but only within 48 hours of arrival. Your passport will be checked before purchases can be made. For **handicrafts**, Baguio offers **woodcarvings** and **weaving**. The best weaving is available at the Easter School of Weaving.

### TOURS AND EXCURSIONS

Tours of many parts of northern Luzon, including hiking in the Mount Pinatubo area, can be arranged through Swagman Travel (offices in Manila, Olongapo, Angeles, Bauang and Baguio). Arrange with your hotel for tours around the SBF.

### USEFUL CONTACTS

**Department of Tourism, Cordillera Administrative Region**, DOT Complex, Governor Pack Rd, Baguio City 2600, tel: 074 619 1127 or 442 7014, e-mail: dotcar@pldtdsl.net
**Regional Office I**, Oasis Country Resort, National Highway, Barangay Sevilla, San Fernando, La Union 2500, tel: 072 888 2411, e-mail: dotregion1@pldtdsl.net
**Regional Office III**, Hilaga Village, San Fernando, Pampanga, tel: 045 477 2499, e-mail: celtour@yahoo.com
**Swagman Travel**, 411 A. Flores St, Ermita, Manila, tel: 02 523 8541, e-mail: bookings@swaggy.com
**Useful websites:**
www.subicbay.com.ph
www.hundredislands.ph
www.batanesonline.com

| BAGUIO | J | F | M | A | M | J | J | A | S | O | N | D |
|---|---|---|---|---|---|---|---|---|---|---|---|---|
| AVERAGE TEMP. °F | 64 | 64 | 66 | 68 | 68 | 68 | 66 | 66 | 68 | 68 | 66 | 64 |
| AVERAGE TEMP. °C | 18 | 18 | 19 | 20 | 20 | 20 | 20 | 19 | 19 | 20 | 19 | 18 |
| RAINFALL in | 0.5 | 0.3 | 1 | 3.5 | 13.6 | 19 | 31.8 | 36 | 24.8 | 14.6 | 4.6 | 0.9 |
| RAINFALL mm | 12 | 8 | 26 | 89 | 346 | 484 | 808 | 912 | 628 | 371 | 116 | 23 |
| DAYS OF RAINFALL | 3 | 2 | 4 | 9 | 19 | 22 | 26 | 28 | 24 | 16 | 8 | 4 |

# 4
# Southern Luzon and Mindoro

Southern Luzon consists of a narrow peninsula stretching for over 600km (375 miles) southeastwards from Manila. It is a highly volcanic land, with several active volcanoes – including both **Taal** and **Mayon**, the country's most active and dangerous volcanoes – and innumerable others that are dormant. Taal stands at the centre of **Calabarzon**, an area just south of Manila that is a weekend playground for Manila residents. Here can be found hiking trails, hot springs, waterfalls and beaches, all within easy reach of the capital.

Mount Mayon is the dominant feature of the **Bicol** region, close to the southeastern tip of Luzon, and it looms ominously over the city of **Legaspi**. Its near-perfect cone, which sweeps upwards from the sea to a pointed smouldering peak, is one of the most recognizable images of the Philippines, and for hikers a climb to its summit is one of the country's greatest challenges. There are a number of other climbable volcanoes in the area, including **Mount Bulusan**. On Luzon's southern coast, **Donsol** has become a mecca for those wishing to see and swim with whale sharks.

Mindoro is a wild and mountainous island to the south of Luzon, easily accessible from Calabarzon. Much of the island is still poorly developed, and tourism concentrates around the resort of **Puerto Galera**, a beautiful peninsula at the northern tip. Off Mindoro's west coast lies **Apo Reef**, an important site for turtles and other marine life, which in recent years has become a popular site for divers.

## DON'T MISS

**\*\*\* Puerto Galera:** coves and beaches, superb diving.
**\*\* Mount Mayon:** the most active volcano in the Philippines, famous for its almost perfect cone.
**\*\* Mount Bulusan:** an active volcano, with a pleasant lake and rainforest at its feet.
**\*\* Los Banos and Mt Makiling:** views of Laguna de Bay, walks in Makiling's forest, and the Philippine Raptor Center.
**\* Lake Taal and Taal Volcano:** views of the caldera lake and the island on which the Taal volcano sits.

**Opposite:** *Even in downtown Legaspi you can see the summit of Mt Mayon.*

**Right:** *Lake Taal, a huge flooded volcanic caldera, presents an idyllic view from Tagaytay high up on the caldera's rim. Taal Island, however, in the centre of the view, is the site of one of the Philippines' most deadly and most active volcanoes.*

## CLIMATE

Calabarzon, the area just south of Manila, and western Mindoro are dry from November to May, and wet June to October. Puerto Galera and Legaspi do not have a completely dry season, but most rain falls November–January. All areas are driest in **April–May** – the hottest months.

## CALABARZON

Calabarzon – an acronym for the provinces of Cavite, Laguna, Batangas, Rizal and Quezon – is a densely populated region immediately to the south of Manila. A large proportion of it is covered by **Laguna de Bay**, the country's largest lake. Waterfalls and hot springs are dotted around the area's mountains, while along the coasts are numerous beaches and dive sites.

## Tagaytay and Taal Volcano ★★

Some 70km (45 miles) south of central Manila lies Taal Lake, a flooded caldera that forms the remains of an ancient massive volcano. In the centre of the lake is an island on which stands Taal volcano, said to be one of the world's smallest but deadliest volcanoes. The lake was once an enclosed bay on the coast, but a series of eruptions in the 18th century sealed the entrance and turned it into a lake. The last big eruption took place in 1911.

For a spectacular view of the lake and volcano island, head for **Tagaytay**, a town on the northwestern rim of the caldera. At an altitude of 760m (2500ft), night time can be especially cool. The town is spread out, and in itself not very interesting. Apart from the view, there is horse riding and also a golf course, while the local volcanology unit has an interesting exhibition.

Boat trips across the lake and hiking on the volcano island, right down into the active crater (where there is another small lake), can be organized at the little towns of Talisay, Leynes or Laurel on the lake's northern shore, or San Nicolas on the south side.

## Los Banos and Mount Makiling ★★

The hot spring resort of Los Banos lies approximately 65km (40 miles) south of Manila, on the southern shore of Laguna de Bay and at the northern foot of Mount Makiling. Hot springs bubbling out from the base of this inactive volcano are the attraction for many Filipinos, and there are a number of resorts scattered along the main road towards Manila. The old part of the town is a quiet, pleasant collection of old houses, with lovely views of the lake and the thousands of fish farms that reach out over the shallow waters.

Above the town, on the lower

> **THE TAAL ERUPTION OF 1911**
>
> One of Taal's worst eruptions in recent history began on 29 January 1911, sending a column of smoke and ash high into the sky, and avalanches of volcanic rock and debris across Taal Island. Many of the farmers tilling the island's rich volcanic soils were killed by the blast, while those that escaped on their boats were drowned by tidal waves that swept the lake. Over 1300 people died on that one day.

**Below:** *The Crested Serpent-Eagle is spread across much of south and Southeast Asia. In the Philippines it is quite a common sight.*

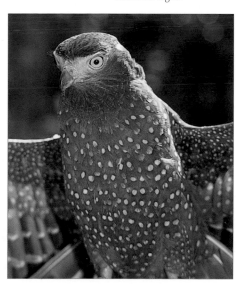

slopes of Makiling, stands a campus of the **University of the Philippines**, housing mostly forestry, agricultural and biology departments. The surroundings are beautiful, with parklands covered with rainforest trees. On the campus is the **Makiling Botanical Garden**, which consists mostly of dense rainforest through which a few roads and many footpaths have been cut. Among the trees is the **Philippine Raptor Center**, a home for injured or confiscated Philippine birds of prey. Besides an extremely tame Crested Serpent-Eagle, this place provides a very rare opportunity to see the world's second-largest raptor, the **Philippine eagle**, of which three live here.

Above the Botanical Garden the campus road becomes a track that climbs the mountain to its summit at 1144m (3752ft). If taking this route, be sure to take plenty of water with you and also to register with the guard at the start of the track. The hike up and down takes all day and is through dense rainforest. Though now classed as a forest reserve, Mount Makiling was one of the country's first national parks, declared in 1933 and protected by the university ever since.

### Mount Banahaw ★★

Southeast of Laguna de Bay stands Mount Banahaw, an active volcano that, with its three peaks and impressive height of 2177m (7141ft), easily dominates the landscape. Partially forested, the mountain has a number of hot

**Right:** *Fish farms and traps spread across the shallow waters of Laguna de Bay, lit by the light of sunrise and seen from Los Banos on the southern shore. The country's largest lake, it is intensively used by the huge local population (which includes parts of Manila), with both pollution and fishing threatening the lake's survival.*

**Left:** Tubastraea *cup corals put on a golden show on a reef near Maricaban Island off the Calumpan Peninsula, Batangas. This area, reached via dive centres in the village of Anilao, offers Manila's nearest good-quality diving.*

springs, waterfalls and caves, and has become known as a sacred mountain. During Holy Week, just before Easter, thousands of people make a pilgrimage to the summit.

There are several trails up the mountain, each making for one of the three peaks, though the most used route starts from the town of San Pablo, on the mountain's northwestern flank. You will need to take all your own equipment and food, and hire a guide at the national park office in the village of Santa Lucia at the trailhead. To the summit and back is an arduous three-day trek.

### Beaches and Dive Resorts ★

About 40km (25 miles) west of Tagaytay, some 110km (70 miles) from Manila, are the towns of **Nasugbu** and **Matabungkay**, the nearest beaches to the capital. Although not the country's most beautiful beaches, they are perfectly enjoyable, with several kilometres of sand, and are easily reached by road.

For diving it is better to head further south, especially to the **Calumpan Peninsula** near Batangas, where most dive resorts are centred around the village of **Anilao**. Here, and most especially around the nearby island of Maricaban, is some excellent diving, with a wealth of coral and fish species to be seen. Note that Anilao has no beach and there is very little for non-divers to do.

### VOLCANOLOGY

The Philippines' volcanoes are studied and monitored by the Philippine Institute of Volcanology and Seismology (PHIVOLCS), based in Manila. Monitoring stations set up close to several of the country's 22 active volcanoes watch for possible eruptions through measurements of localized earthquake activity and gas emissions. Increasing numbers of earthquakes, which come progressively closer to the earth's surface and more closely aligned with the volcano's base, are a clear indication of an approaching eruption. Knowing exactly when the eruption will take place, however, is still extremely difficult to predict.

**Right:** *Teeing off across a ravine at the Ponderosa Golf Club, in the hills high above Puerto Galera.*
**Opposite:** *Boats drawn up on the sand at Big La Laguna Beach, Puerto Galera, Mindoro.*

## KING COCONUT

It is hard to find a crop more versatile than the coconut palm. Drinking its milk and eating its flesh are just the tip of the iceberg. Not only is the tree itself valuable for construction materials, but the nuts have a huge range of uses. These include the production of coconut oils, copra, charcoal, activated carbon, vinegar, plant culture media, growth hormones, laundry soap and detergent. Coconut is a major crop in the Philippines, an estimated 331 million palms occupying 3.25 million hectares (8 million acres), or 27% of the country's farmland. The country's palms account for a huge proportion of the world's coconut oil, about 1.6 million tonnes exported annually.

## MINDORO

This wild and mountainous island has been little explored by visitors, and although a trickle of divers head for the west coast town of **Sablayan** in order to reach the dive sites of **Apo Reef**, the great majority of visitors head for just one place – **Puerto Galera** – situated at the northernmost tip of Mindoro.

## Puerto Galera ★★★

A two-hour ferry journey from the port of Batangas on the southern tip of Calabarzon, Puerto Galera is one of the Philippines' most popular and most beautiful resort areas. Upon arrival from Batangas, the ferry enters **Muelle Bay**, a landlocked stretch of water enclosed by a peninsula and a cluster of islands, all vivid green in their covering of coconut palms. Sandy beaches line the shore and yachts lie at anchor close to the wharf that marks arrival at Puerto Galera town. From here, new arrivals are taken by *bangka* or jeepney out to any one of numerous beaches lying east and west of the town.

The most popular destinations in the area are the beaches at **Big** and **Small La Laguna** and **Sabang**, which line the outermost point of the Puerto Galera Peninsula to the east of town. To the west lie several more beaches, including **White Beach**, **Aninuan** and **Talipanan**, which are generally less developed than the first three. Puerto Galera is one of the country's prime dive sites, a large area of coral reefs having been protected in a **marine sanctuary** for many years. There is a great array of hard and soft corals, basket sponges, sea fans and fish life, and the many dive operators all offer training courses.

Inland, there is a **golf course**, a remarkable place hacked out of the steep terrain and dense forests, which at one point involves teeing off across a ravine. There are also a couple of waterfalls, both within walking distance of Talipanan and Aninuan beaches, while longer hikes lead to villages inhabited by the **Mangyan** people, Mindoro's aboriginals.

### PUERTO GALERA DIVE SITES

Most of the best dive sites are within or close to the marine reserve, which stretches along the northern coastline of the peninsula. Some of the dives are over shallow coral gardens that snorkellers can enjoy too, but others are deep and in some places involve strong currents. On the shallower dives a wide range of corals, basket sponges and reef fish can be seen. In the deepest waters, at around 40m (130ft), sharks may be encountered. There are at least 24 dive sites, with names as varied as Manila Channel, Monkey Wreck, Sabang Point, Ernie's Cave, Hole in the Wall and The Fish Bowl.

### Apo Reef **

Lying about 35km (20 miles) off the west coast of Mindoro, Apo Reef is a national park, protected for its importance to nesting turtles. Occupying an area of about 15,800ha (57 sq miles), the reef contains three small islets, the largest of which, Apo Island, is surrounded by mangroves.

The reef is also of great interest to divers and underwater photographers as, surrounded by extremely deep waters, it teems with a great diversity of life. Dive safaris are often organized from Puerto Galera during the calm months of April–May, though a much closer access point is the town of Sablayan, on Mindoro's west coast. There is also good diving available here, around **Pandan Island**, a few kilometres offshore.

## MAYON MYTHOLOGY

According to mythology Mount Mayon arose on the spot where two lovers, a prince called Ulap and a princess named Daragang Magayon, were buried. It is said they were killed in a battle caused by a jealous suitor, Pagtuga. Incensed that Ulap, a stranger from another part of Luzon, was to be allowed to marry Magayon, Pagtuga had kidnapped the princess's father, demanding that she marry him. Pagtuga was killed in the ensuing battle, as well as the two lovers. Apparently, when the tip of the volcano is covered with cloud Ulap is kissing Magayon. When it is raining, he is crying.

**Below:** *Watching out for the whale sharks of Donsol. The discovery of a resident population has excited marine biologists and triggered both a scramble to ensure their protection and a boom in local tourism.*

## THE FAR SOUTH

The far south of Luzon, known as **Bicol**, is an intensely volcanic landscape, dominated by the active volcanoes **Mayon** and **Bulusan**.

### Legaspi ★

Also spelled Legazpi, this port is the largest city in the far south of Luzon. Even so, it is still a small place and one that would have very little interest for the visitor were it not for the huge conical shape of Mount Mayon looming over it. One of the best views can be obtained from the top of **Kapuntukan Hill**, on the coast south of the port.

About 6km (4 miles) northwest of Legaspi are the **Cagsawa Ruins**. Here stands a ruined church, all that remains of a village buried by lava flows following a major eruption in 1814. A further 5km (3 miles) northwest of Cagsawa is Camalig, right at the foot of the volcano, and site of the **Hoyop-Hoyopan Cave**. Though there are various limestone caves in the area, this is the most accessible. A complex of passages filled with stalactites and stalagmites, the cave usually has a cooling wind blowing through its chambers.

There are a number of waterfalls in the area, one of the most accessible being **Busay Falls** near Malilipot, on the northeastern edge of Mount Mayon. This beautiful waterfall has seven levels, with a pool at the base of each leading into the next level below.

### Mount Mayon ★★

At 2421m (7941ft) Mayon is famous for being the Philippines' most active volcano and for its almost perfect conical shape. The volcano is known to have erupted 48 times, most recently in 2000, 2001 and again in 2006. During each, thousands of people were evacuated from the area.

For the non-hiker the closest view of the mountain is from its northern slope: the **Mayon Skyline Hotel** at an altitude of 760m (2500ft). From here there are stunning views of the surrounding countryside and nearby coast.

To climb Mayon, the trail starts on the southern slope from the village of Buyuan. You will need to take all your own equipment and food, and hire a guide. Make arrangements with the Department of Tourism in Legaspi. Remember that the mountain is constantly active and from time to time is closed due to the danger of an eruption.

**Above:** *Mount Mayon is infamous for its frequent eruptions and the fact that the port city of Legaspi sits rather close to its base.*

### Sorsogon **

The two most important attractions of Sorsogon are **Mount Bulusan** and the whale sharks of **Donsol**.

At Donsol, a fishing town 40km (25 miles) south of Legaspi, a whale shark watching operation has been set up, where visitors can hire a boat and tour the bay to see these gentle giants. Sightings of the fish right at the surface are almost guaranteed, and if you have a mask and snorkel it is possible to swim alongside them. The best time to go is early morning, January–May.

About 80km (50 miles) southeast of Legaspi is Bicol's second active volcano, Mount Bulusan. Surrounded by a 3673ha (9182-acre) national park, many of Bulusan's slopes are cloaked in healthy rainforest, especially in the area around **Bulusan Lake**, a delightful place to explore and one which still has plenty of wildlife. A trail leads up to the summit at 1559m (5114ft) from near the village of San Roque, on the southern side. As for Mayon, you need to take a guide plus all your own food and equipment, and pay attention to eruption warnings. Make arrangements with the provincial tourism council in Sorsogon town.

---

**WHALE SHARKS**

This is the world's largest fish, measuring up to 15m (50ft) in length. Being a plankton feeder, however, it is quite harmless. Little is known of its behaviour, but it is thought to be quite rare. Australian researchers normally have to use spotter planes to find any around their coasts, and they count themselves lucky to find 10 in a week. So it came as a big surprise when conservationists discovered a concentration of perhaps as many as 50 in a small area off Donsol. For many years local fishermen had known of them, but it was not until the end of 1997 that the news got out. Now there is a big drive to study their behaviour and ensure that they are protected.

## Southern Luzon and Mindoro at a Glance

BEST TIMES TO VISIT

For all parts of this region the driest months are Mar–May, although Puerto Galera and Legaspi do not have a truly dry season, unlike Calabarzon and western Mindoro. For Puerto Galera and Legaspi the heaviest rain is from Nov–Jan, whereas for western Mindoro and Calabarzon this occurs in Jun–Oct. Due to rough seas, Apo Reef is generally accessible only from Mar–May.

GETTING THERE

Regular **bus** services link Manila to many parts of Calabarzon. To reach Puerto Galera, a combined **bus/ferry** ticket can be bought in Manila, with buses leaving the City State Tower Hotel in Ermita every morning. The journey takes about five hours. For Sablayan, fly to San José on Mindoro's west coast, and then travel by bus, or take an overnight ferry from Batangas to Sablayan. For Bicol, there are daily **flights** to Legaspi, as well as **buses** and **trains**.

GETTING AROUND

In Calabarzon most of the **bus** services run between Manila and specific points, so getting around from place to place within the region can be quite difficult, requiring multiple **jeepney** rides. Self-drive **car hire** from Manila is an option, made a little difficult by the lack of signposting. In Puerto

Galera, most transport is by **boat**, though there are jeepneys in some areas. The west coast of Mindoro has a rough road that is travelled by jeepneys and buses. In Bicol frequent buses link Legaspi with Sorsogon and also the Mount Bulusan area. To get into the Bulusan Volcano National Park, hire a jeepney in Irosin. Donsol is most easily reached by taking a jeepney directly from Legaspi.

WHERE TO STAY

### Tagaytay
*LUXURY*
**Taal Vista Hotel**, Km 60, Aguinaldo Highway, Tagaytay City, Cavite, tel: 046 413 1000, e-mail: sales@taalvista hotel.com web: www.taalvista hotel.com Manila booking office: Ground Floor, One E-com Center, Harbor Drive, Mall of Asia Complex CBP-1A, Pasay City 1300, Metro Manila, tel: 02 403 1000. The best hotel in Tagaytay; on the edge of the Taal caldera; spectacular views across the lake and volcano island.

### Los Banos
*MID-RANGE*
**City of Springs Resort Hotel**, 147 N Villegas St, Los Banos, Laguna 4030, tel: 049 536 0731, web: www.splash mountain.com Pleasant hotel in old part of Los Banos, right on the shores of Laguna de Bay, with a range of room types, a swimming pool, natural spring, and restaurant.

### Puerto Galera
*MID-RANGE*
**La Laguna Beach Club and Dive Centre**, Big La Laguna Beach, Puerto Galera, Oriental Mindoro 5203, tel: 043 287 3181, cell: 0917 794 0323, e-mail: lalaguna@llbc.com.ph web: www.llbcdiveresort.com or www.llbc.com.ph
**El Galleon Beach Resort**, Small La Laguna Beach, Puerto Galera, Oriental Mindoro, tel: 043 287 3205, cell: 0917 814 5107, e-mail: admin@asia divers.com web: www.asia divers.com/elgalleon
**Marco Vincent Resort**, White Beach, Puerto Galera, Oriental Mindoro 5203. Manila office: Unit 503, Cityland 10, Tower 1, 156 HV Dela Costa cnr Ayala Ave, Makati, Metro Manila, tel: 02 813 6329, e-mail: reservation@marco vincent.com web: www. marcovincent.com

### Sablayan
*BUDGET*
**Pandan Island Resort**, Pandan Island, 5104 Sablayan, Occidental Mindoro, tel (cell): 0919 305 7821, e-mail: info@pandan. com web: www.pandan.com Manila tel: 02 523 7007.

### Legaspi
*LUXURY*
**Hotel Venezia**, Renaissance Gardens, Washington Drive, Legaspi City, Albay, tel: 052 481 0877, e-mail: hvrsvn@ discovery.com.ph web: www.hotelvenezia.com.ph Manila tel: 02 683 8222.

*MID-RANGE*

**Hotel La Trinidad**, Rizal St, Legaspi City, Albay, tel: 052 480 7469, fax: 052 481 4444. A city centre hotel with an interesting restaurant.

**Casablanca Hotel**, 185 Peña-randa St, Legaspi City, Albay, tel: 052 480 8334, fax: 052 480 8338, e-mail: info@ casablancahotel.ph web: www.casablancahotel.ph Near city centre; excellent Chinese restaurant.

*Sorsogon*

*MID-RANGE*

**Fernandos Hotel**, N Pareja St, Bitan-o, Sorsogon City, tel: 056 211 1357, fax: 056 211 1537, e-mail: fernando hotel@hotmail.com web: www.sorsogontourism.com/ fernandos.htm Family-run hotel with garden and the best restaurant in town. Also the headquarters for the Provincial Tourism Council.

### WHERE TO EAT

The best (and often the only) places to eat are in your own hotel or resort. Additional recommendations:

*Puerto Galera*

**Portofino Restaurant**, Portofino Beach Resort, Small La Laguna Beach, Puerto Galera, Oriental Mindoro 5203, tel/fax: 043 287 3227, e-mail: resort@portofino.com.ph web: www.portofino.com.ph Western and Filipino food.

**Fishermen's Cove**, Sto Nino, Puerto Galera, Oriental

Mindoro, tel (cell): 0917 533 2985. An Italian restaurant and beach resort close to Puerto Galera.

**Relax Thai Restaurant**, Sabang, Puerto Galera, Oriental Mindoro, tel (cell): 0973 878 781, e-mail: thaimonk@ mindoro.net Centre of Sabang Village; excellent Thai food.

*Legaspi*

**Orient Garden**, Casablanca Hotel, Peñaranda St, Legaspi City, Albay, tel: 052 480 8334. An excellent, if slightly expensive, Chinese restaurant inside this hotel.

### TOURS AND EXCURSIONS

Tours of the Calabarzon region can generally be arranged by your Manila hotel. Alternatively, self-drive car hire is easily arranged. In Puerto Galera, to make tours of the coast or to inland areas, make arrangements with your own resort. Tours around the Mount Mayon and Legaspi areas can be arranged with the local office of the Department of Tourism. This office should also be approached for help in organizing a climb up the volcano. Visits to Bulusan Volcano National Park can be

arranged through the Sorsogon Provincial Tourism Council.

### SPORTS

Main sports are **diving** and **hiking**, the former at Anilao, Puerto Galera, Pandan Island and Apo Reef. The best hiking areas are Taal volcano island, Mount Banahaw, Mount Makiling, Mount Mayon and Mount Bulusan.

### USEFUL CONTACTS

**Department of Tourism**, **Regional Office IV**, Rm 208, DOT Bldg, TM Kalaw St, Ermita, Manila 1000, tel: 02 524 1969 or 542 1528, e-mail: lcjurilla@tourism.gov.ph **Regional Office V**, Regional Center Site, Rawis, Legazpi City 4500, tel: 052 481 5593, e-mail: dot_bicol@yahoo.com **Sorsogon Provincial Tourism Council**, N Pareja St, Bitan-o, Sorsogon City, tel: 056 211 1357, fax: 056 211 1537, e-mail: chairsptc@hotmail.com **Useful websites:** www.puerto-galera-resorts.s5.com and www. puertogalera.ph For accommo-dation in Puerto Galera. www.sorsogontourism.com and www.wowbicol.com Tourism websites for the far south of Luzon.

| LEGASPI | J | F | M | A | M | J | J | A | S | O | N | D |
|---|---|---|---|---|---|---|---|---|---|---|---|---|
| AVERAGE TEMP. °F | 77 | 79 | 79 | 81 | 82 | 82 | 81 | 82 | 82 | 81 | 81 | 79 |
| AVERAGE TEMP. °C | 25 | 26 | 26 | 27 | 28 | 28 | 27 | 28 | 28 | 27 | 27 | 79 |
| RAINFALL in | 11.8 | 7 | 6.4 | 6.1 | 6.5 | 9.9 | 11.3 | 10.4 | 10.6 | 12.6 | 18.7 | 20 |
| RAINFALL mm | 301 | 179 | 163 | 155 | 166 | 252 | 287 | 265 | 270 | 320 | 475 | 508 |
| DAYS OF RAINFALL | 21 | 15 | 16 | 15 | 14 | 16 | 20 | 18 | 20 | 21 | 22 | 23 |

# 5
# Western Visayas

The Visayas form the archipelago that makes up the fractured waist of the Philippines. This is the area where the country's best beaches are situated and where island-hopping is a daily part of life. When people think of the Philippines, it is often specifically the Visayas that spring to mind.

The western Visayas contain the main islands of **Negros** and **Panay**, along with a host of smaller ones that include **Boracay**, home to one of Southeast Asia's most spectacular beaches and the Philippines' number one attraction. Boracay's nearest major town is **Kalibo**, the site each January of **Ati-Atihan**, perhaps the country's most popular festival. At the southern end of Panay is **Iloilo**, an important port and the largest city in the western Visayas. Site of the country's second-oldest Spanish settlement, the surrounding area contains many Spanish churches. The city itself is a working place, but each January – as is the case in Kalibo – the city explodes into festival with **Dinagyang**.

It is a short hop from Iloilo to Negros and its largest city, **Bacolod**. More than half of the country's sugar cane is grown on Negros, and you can see huge estates devoted to nothing else. Some wild areas have survived, notably **Mount Kanlaon**, the highest mountain in the Visayas, an active volcano surrounded by rainforest. On the east coast, **Dumaguete** is a pleasant university city, with beaches to the south and excellent diving around **Apo Island**. To the north, it is possible to go on whale- and dolphin-watching trips from the town of **Bais**.

## DON'T MISS

**\*\*\* Boracay:** a small island lined with dazzling white beaches; there is also good diving here.
**\*\*\* Ati-Atihan Festival:** held the third weekend of January in Kalibo – a scene of colourful dancing.
**\*\* Bais:** dolphin- and whale-watching in the Tanon Strait.
**\*\* Dumaguete:** a pleasant university town, with lovely beaches nearby.

**Opposite:** *White Beach, several kilometres of white sand, runs along much of the west coast of Boracay, making it one of Southeast Asia's island paradises.*

## CLIMATE

For the whole region rain falls from June to October or November, with dry, sunny weather from November to May. Boracay has occasional showers December–February. The hottest, driest months are **April** and **May**.

## TROPICAL PARADISE

Boracay was first 'discovered' in the late 1970s and early 80s by backpacking travellers in search of the ultimate unspoiled tropical paradise. They found an island that had just a couple of fishing communities and one of the most astonishing beaches in Asia. Simple accommodation developed, which by the end of the 1980s stretched along much of White Beach. In the 1990s business started to move up-market, with the construction of an extensive golf course and luxury apartments. Boracay had lost its early innocence and simplicity, and became a major player in the international resort scene.

## BORACAY

The principal area of interest for the visitor in this region is beautiful Boracay Island. At just 7km (4.5 miles) long and less than 1km (600yd) wide at its narrowest point, this little island is the jewel in the Philippines' crown. The main attraction is **White Beach**, 4km (2.5 miles) of blinding white powdery sand along the west coast, lapped by warm, clear water that in the shallows is enticing aquamarine, changing in the greater depths to a deep cobalt blue.

With three main villages – Manoc-Manoc, Balabag and Yapak – the island has a population of about 6500, though during the height of the visitor season (January to April) numbers swell to way above this. The place has been luring visitors in ever-increasing numbers since the early 1980s, and today some would say Boracay has passed saturation point. Small-scale resort developments line virtually the whole of White Beach, and there have been some environmental problems concerning rubbish and sewage, though the locals insist they are getting to grips with this. The north end of the island has seen some huge developments, with the creation of a large golf course and the construction of luxury apartments, something that many people feel has ruined Boracay's simple, rural feeling.

That said, however, Boracay is still a glorious place. Despite the large number of visitors, the beach is big enough to accommodate everyone, ensuring that its relaxed ambience continues. The golf course and the apartment development remain well out of sight several

kilometres away. For those who really do want to get well away from crowds, there are several other lightly used beaches, such as **Diniwid**, just north of White Beach, and **Yapak Beach** at the northern end of the island.

If lazing around on the sand all day is not your kind of thing, there are plenty of other things to do. On land you can hire

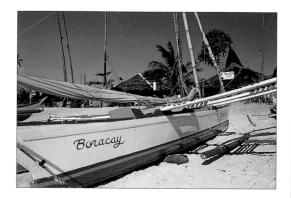

**Left:** *A paraw, or sailing outrigger, pulled up onto the beach; Boracay.*
**Opposite:** *Beach volleyball on Boracay's White Beach.*

### BORACAY'S DIVE SITES

Boracay has plenty of diving facilities, with dive shops scattered along much of the length of White Beach; one of the best is Calypso Diving. Despite dynamite damage to reefs in some areas, Boracay's diving is quite good, and for such a small area remarkably varied. With 12 dive sites immediately around the island itself, and several more further afield, sites vary from coral gardens at a depth of just a few metres (such as Laurel, Crocodile Island and Balinghai Beach) to exciting blue water dives, such as Yapak 1 and 2, which are 35m (115ft) dives onto a ledge where sharks are often seen.

bicycles to explore the island, or you could go horse riding. If cycling sounds a bit too energetic, there are plenty of motorized tricycles to be hired – they are the only form of motor transport on the island. On the water, at White Beach, there are a number of sailing *bangkas* to be hired, outrigger boats that can be very fast and exciting in the right wind, and on the east coast are several **windsurfing** centres.

Inevitably, White Beach is littered with **dive operations**. Boracay's diving is surprisingly good, ranging from coral gardens at reasonably shallow depths to exciting dives into deep blue water where encounters with sharks are quite common.

*Above: Drummers at the colourful Ati-Atihan Festival, held each January.*

### THE TEN DATUS

Kalibo's Ati-Atihan and Iloilo's Dinagyang Festivals, along with a host of other similar events occurring all over Panay in January, celebrate events thought to have taken place in the 13th century and described in a book called the *Maragtas*. It is the tale of the **10 Datus**, Malay chieftains who sailed from Borneo with all their people to escape tyranny there. The story relates that the Malays, led by Datu Puti, landed in the south of Panay where they met the local Negrito chief, Marikudo. Puti bought the land from Marikudo in exchange for gold, and the Malays then spread to different points on Panay, including Kalibo and Iloilo, with some continuing on to the Lake Taal area of Luzon.

## PANAY

A large, triangular island on the western edge of the Visayas, Panay is a mainly rural area which is divided into four provinces. The eastern half of the island consists of lowlands where several crops, mostly sugar cane and rice, are grown. To the west lies a line of high, partially forested mountains, the tallest of which is Mount Madja-as at 2090m (6855ft).

### Kalibo *

Most visitors on their way to or from Boracay pass through Kalibo as this is the destination for the majority of flights between Manila and the region. For most of the year there is little to see in this provincial town. For a couple of weeks each January, however, the town comes alive with its annual festival, **Ati-Atihan**, which culminates on the third weekend of the month in huge dances and parades around town.

The event celebrates agreements struck in the 13th century between the native Aeta people and the immigrating Malays (whose descendants today make up much of Panay's population), who had just crossed from Borneo. In the dances and parades local teams daub their skins black to resemble the early Aeta people and dress in fantastic costumes with intense competition to see which is best. The event is raucous and chaotic, and with zero crowd control this is the ultimate participatory event.

### Iloilo *

With a population of around 350,000 Iloilo is Panay's largest city, situated in the south of the island at the mouth of the Iloilo River and sheltered by the island of Guimaras. Today's city sits close to the site of Spain's second Philippine settlement, established in 1566 but moved to the site of the present city in 1700. For many years the area was a major centre for weaving using locally grown Manila hemp and *piña*, the latter a fibre produced from the pineapple leaf. This died away in the second half of the 19th century, though today there has been a small resurgence. Such weaving can be seen in the suburb of **Arevalo**.

Within the city one place worth a visit is the **Museo Iloilo**, where good displays trace much of the city's history and culture (it is open 09:00–17:00 Mon–Fri). For those who enjoy everyday life, the **port** along the south bank of the Iloilo River is worth exploring, as are the two bustling **markets**.

**Below:** *The Church of Santo Tomas de Villanueva, at Miagao, near Iloilo, Panay, was completed in 1797 and today is a UNESCO World Heritage Site.*

## SUGAR CANE

Cultivation of sugar cane began on Negros in the second half of the 19th century, encouraged by Nicholas Loney, British vice consul in Iloilo, to balance his imports of cheap British textiles. Today, about 383,000ha (946,393 acres) of the Philippines are given over to sugar cane production, much of it on large plantations owned by a few people. Harvest time is from October to April, and this is the time to see the plantations' trains in action, bringing the cane to the sugar mills. Most sugar is produced on Negros, whose 202,000ha (499,142-acre) sugar plantations produce about 22 million tonnes of sugar annually, 53% of the country's output.

**Opposite:** *Hikers descend the lower slopes of Mount Kanlaon, where much of the rainforest has been replaced by farmland.*
**Below:** *The attractive facade of the Negros Occidental Provincial Museum, in Bacolod.*

The suburbs of **Jaro** and **Molo** have attractive Spanish churches, while about 40km (25 miles) to the west **Miagao** has one of the most spectacular. Dating from 1786, this fortress church is a UNESCO World Heritage Site, perhaps due to the superb frieze on the walls above the main entrance, showing a mixture of European figures and tropical vegetation. Still further west the church at **San Joaquin** has a façade recalling the 1859 Spanish–Muslim battle at Tetuan, Morocco.

The main reason to come to Iloilo is to experience the **Dinagyang Festival**, held one week after Kalibo's Ati-Atihan, and similar in style and origins. Another spectacularly colourful event, Iloilo's festival is much more controlled than that of Kalibo, with lavish and highly choreographed dance routines. You have to watch the dancing from a viewing stand.

## NEGROS

Negros is a rectangular island, divided along its length by a line of mountains containing six volcanoes, only one of which – Mount Kanlaon – is presently active. The main product is sugar, introduced in the second half of the 19th century. The resulting plantation economy has fostered an immensely wealthy and powerful elite who own the vast sugar *haciendas*. A slump in sugar prices a few years ago caused considerable hardship to the workers, and the island is now attempting to diversify its economy, with increased tourism a major goal.

### Bacolod *

Located on the west coast of Negros, Bacolod is the island's largest city. It has little for the visitor, although the **Provincial Museum** has some excellent displays. The city is, however, a good base from which to explore the area. Several **sugar plantations** can be toured during the cutting season (October–April), and these are especially interesting for their own narrow-gauge railways that bring the sugar cane from the fields to the mills.

To the north of Bacolod the town of **Silay** is known for its old villas, remnants of an era when this was a major port and those who had grown rich on sugar lived here. Inland from the town you can climb into the hills of **Patag**. There are extensive hiking trails here, and for lovers of beautiful waterfalls it is heaven.

Inland from Bacolod is **Mambucal**, a hot spring resort at the feet of Mount Kanlaon, Negros's only active volcano. The resort is a little rundown, but occupies a lovely spot surrounded by trees, and the baths are hot and relaxing.

### Mount Kanlaon ★★

At 2465m (8085ft) this is the highest mountain in the Visayas and, surrounded by dense rainforest, it is one of the country's most important national parks. On the Bacolod side, trails climb up from Mambucal in the north and the tiny village of **Guintubdan** on the western slopes. A hike from one to the other takes three days.

Make arrangements with the tourism office in Bacolod, where you can pick up guides and porters. Obtain a permit from the national park office in the city, and buy all your supplies before setting off. Take heed of warnings of volcanic activity – Kanlaon last erupted in 2006, but frequently shows activity, from small earthquakes to ash clouds and minor explosions.

### A CLIMB UP MOUNT KANLAON

One of the best routes is to start at the little village of Guintubdan and finish at the hot spring resort of Mambucal. At Guintubdan permits are checked, and from here the hike is a steep climb through dense rainforest all the way to the summit. There are two campsites en route: spending the first night at Camp 2 ensures that the summit can be reached within two hours the next morning. Just before the summit the forest ends, and there is an old crater, now green and pleasant. At the summit is the active crater, a gaping hole with sheer walls. From the summit to Mambucal is a two-day hike, with a night's camping next to a pretty lake. There is dense forest all the way, and you pass several lakes – the remains of ancient craters. Much of the lower (dipterocarp) forest has been lost, especially around a new geothermal plant. From here it seems to take a long time to reach Mambucal, but when you do the hot spring bath makes it all worthwhile!

**Right:** *The weekly market at Malatapay, south of Dumaguete, is a colourful and lively affair, well worth visiting for the opportunity it presents to enjoy a slice of rural life.*

At Guintubdan, where permits are checked, you are already in the forest. It is a steep climb for 1½ days to the summit through very dense forest. The summit has a terrifying crater that plunges straight down into the bowels of the earth, and there are stupendous views across Negros to Panay and Cebu. From the summit to Mambucal is a two-day hike passing several lakes that are extinct craters. The last part of the trail passes a geothermal plant, and after an exhausting climb over a final spur you descend into Mambucal.

### Bais ★★

A pleasant town towards the southern end of the island, Bais is the place to arrange boat trips to watch dolphins and whales in the nearby **Tanon Strait**, a narrow but incredibly deep stretch of water separating Negros from Cebu. Boats can be arranged through the tourism office. Trips last up to six hours, with sightings virtually guaranteed. You will almost certainly encounter dolphins, since so many live permanently in this part of the strait. Most common are spinner dolphins, but there are also several other species of dolphin, as well as pilot whales and pygmy sperm whales. The really big whales are rarely seen in this confined piece of water.

### Dumaguete ★★

This is an attractive university city on the island's southeast coast. The leafy campus of **Silliman University** takes up a sizeable chunk of the town, while on the northern

---

### CenTrop

The Center for Tropical Conservation Studies was set up in Dumaguete in 1989 to study and conserve the Philippines' native habitats and wildlife. Its headquarters is in an area called the mini-forest in the north of the city, where they have a captive breeding programme for a number of endangered species, including the Philippine spotted deer, the Visayan warty pig and the leopard cat. They also have a captive breeding facility for several species of endangered fruit bat.

edge is **Silliman Marine Laboratory**, one of the most important centres for marine biology research in Southeast Asia. Also in the northern part of town is **CenTrop**, the Center for Tropical Conservation Studies, where a zoo-cum-captive breeding centre keeps a number of endangered mammals that are unique to the Philippines. On the main part of the university campus close to the city centre is an excellent **Anthropology Museum**, with displays of both archaeological finds and the lives of the Philippines' indigenous peoples.

### Around Dumaguete **

Looming over Dumaguete is **Cuernos de Negros,** a twin-peaked mountain that is still covered with primary rainforest. One of the peaks, **Mount Talinis**, can be climbed, the trail requiring just a few hours from the road head. Make arrangements with the tourist office. Northeast of Talinis is **Lake Balinsasayao**, a beautiful place surrounded by the same rainforest. Access is along a treacherous track that is passable only for four-wheel-drive vehicles.

Along the coast south of Dumaguete are some good beaches, principally at the little town of **Dauin**, 13km (8 miles) to the south of the city. There are a number of pleasant resorts here, which offer diving around nearby **Apo Island**. A marine sanctuary under the protection of the Silliman Marine Laboratory, the reefs around this island are of major importance to conservation. Diving here reveals a huge wealth of coral and fish life, but take great care as the currents can be extremely strong.

About 1000 people live on Apo Island and there is also one resort here. The island can be reached by boat from **Malatapay**, a few kilometres south of Dauin. It is interesting for its Wednesday morning market, a colourful country event of handicrafts, produce and livestock.

---

**DIVING AROUND APO ISLAND**

Not to be confused with Apo Reef off the west coast of Mindoro, the reefs around this little island near Dumaguete have been protected by Silliman University's Marine Laboratory since the 1970s. The result is that the reefs here are intact and offer superb diving. Also, being surrounded by deep water, shoals of larger fish such as barracuda, jack and tuna are common. Giant clams and barrel sponges are widespread, along with gorgonian sea fans and a range of hard and soft coral species. Be warned that currents here can be fierce.

**Below:** *Aboard a dive boat, a diving instructor watches the approach to Apo Island, a popular diving site and an important marine reserve off the southern tip of Negros.*

## Western Visayas at a Glance

The rainy season is Jun–Dec, the dry Jan–May. The hottest months are Apr–May. Catch the Ati-Atihan and Dinagyang festivals in Panay in **January**. Do not climb any mountains during the rainy season.

Daily **flights** connect Manila to Caticlan, Iloilo, Kalibo and Bacolod, and frequent flights go to these places from Cebu. Only small planes fly to Caticlan, so most people going to Boracay fly to Kalibo. Special air-conditioned **buses** run from Kalibo airport to the ferry pier at Caticlan. Frequent *bangkas* serve as **ferries** between Caticlan and Boracay's White Beach. There is no wharf at White Beach, so you have to wade ashore. Ferries run from Manila and Cebu City to Iloilo and Bacolod. A ferry connects Manila with New Washington, which serves Kalibo. Frequent high-speed ferries run between Cebu City and Dumaguete.

On Boracay transport is by **motorized tricycle** or **bicycle**. Airport shuttle **buses**, regular **jeepneys** and air-conditioned **minibuses** run between Caticlan and downtown Kalibo. Buses and faster, more comfortable minibuses travel between Kalibo and Iloilo. Several daily high-speed **ferries** go between Iloilo and Bacolod. On Negros, jeepneys link Bacolod to Silay and Mambucal. For Guintub-

dan, take a shuttle bus to La Carlota, then a jeepney. Buses, some air conditioned, run frequently between Bacolod and Dumaguete. Buses link Dumaguete with Malatapay, Dauin and Bais. You need to hire a vehicle to reach Mount Talinis and Lake Balinsasayao.

### Boracay
*LUXURY*
**Friday's Beach Resort**, Boracay Island, Malay 5608, Aklan, tel: 036 288 6200, e-mail: reservations@fridaysboracay. com www.fridaysboracay.com Manila tel: 02 892 9283. Northern end of White Beach.
*MID-RANGE*
**Tonglen Beach Resort**, Manggayad, Boracay Island, Aklan, tel: 036 288 3457, fax: 036 288 3919, e-mail: tonglen resort@yahoo.com web: www.boracaytonglen.com Five minutes from White Beach; air-con; restaurant.
**The A-Rock Resort**, Boat no 3, Ambulong, Boracay Island, Aklan, tel: 036 288 3201, fax: 036 288 3201, e-mail: arockresort@yahoo.com.ph South end of White Beach.
**Pinjalo Resort Villas**, Boracay Island, Malay 5608, Aklan, tel: 036 288 3206, e-mail: info@ pinjalo.com web: www.pin jalo.com Collection of villas two mins from White Beach, linked with Calypso Diving.

### Iloilo
*LUXURY*
**Days Hotel Iloilo**, 4/F, The

Atrium Mall, General Luna St, Iloilo City 5000, tel: 033 337 3297, fax: 033 336 8000, e-mail: reservations@dayshotel worldwide.com web: www. daysinn.com Built over an indoor shopping mall.
*MID-RANGE*
**Amigo Terrace Hotel**, cnr Iznart & Delgado Sts, Iloilo City 5000, tel: 033 335 0908, fax: 033 335 0610, e-mail: amigo terrace@yahoo.com web: www.amigoterracehotel-iloilo. com Modern, comfortable.
**Four Season Hotel**, cnr Fuentes and Delgado Sts, Iloilo City 5000, tel: 033 336 1070, e-mail: info@four-seasonhotel. com.ph web: www.four-seasonhotel.com.ph

### Dumaguete
*MID-RANGE*
**Bethel Guest House**, Rizal Boulevard, Dumaguete City, Oriental Negros, tel: 035 225 2000, web: www.bethelguest house.com
**El Dorado Beach Resort**, Dauin, nr Dumaguete, Oriental Negros, tel: 035 425 2274, fax: 035 424 0238, e-mail: info@ eldoradobeachresort.com web: www.eldoradobeachresort.com

### Bacolod
*LUXURY*
**Luxur Place Hotel**, Magsaysay Ave, cnr Lacson St, Bacolod City, tel: 034 434 4551, fax: 034 433 3757, web: www. luxurplace-bacolod.com Air conditioned; with restaurant.
*MID-RANGE*
**Sugarland Hotel**, Araneta St,

# Western Visayas at a Glance

Singcang, Bacolod City, tel: 034 435 2690, fax: 034 435 2645, e-mail: contact@sugar landhotel.com web: www. sugarlandhotel.com Modern, air-conditioned hotel.
**Prominence Inn**, 158 C Philsu-gin Rd, Bacolod City, tel: 034 435 0021, e-mail: prominence @mozcom.com Guesthouse with restaurant and garden.

## WHERE TO EAT

### Boracay
**Chez de Paris**, Boracay Island, Malay, Aklan, tel: 036 288 3233, e-mail: deparisroger@ netscape.net web: www. deparis.8m.com Fine French and east Asian cuisine.
**Bamboo Restaurant**, Mang-gayad, Boracay Island, Aklan, tel: 036 288 3109, e-mail: bamboo_resort@yahoo.com web: www.bambooboracay. com.ph Fixed-price buffet, superb seafood.
**Sulu Bar**, Angol, Boracay Island, Aklan, tel: 036 288 3400, e-mail: info@sulu-plaza.com web: www.sulu-plaza.com Thai food.
**English Bakery and Tea Room**, Bolobog Rd, Balabag, Boracay, Aklan, tel: 036 288 3158. Fish and chips, pasties, English tea.

### Iloilo
**Afrique's**, 107 Castilla St, Jaro, Iloilo City 5000, tel: 033 509 2811. Italian food.

### Dumaguete
**New Chin Loong**, 2 Rizal Bou-levard, Dumaguete City, tel: 035 225 4491. Chinese food.

**Casablanca**, 142 Cervantes St, cnr Colon Extension, Duma-guete City, tel: 035 422 4080, e-mail: guesanin@gmail.com

### Bacolod
**Café Uma**, Cnr 15th & Lacson Sts, Bacolod City, tel: 034 709 9966, e-mail: info@cafeuma. com web: www.cafeuma.com Western food with Italian slant.

## TOURS AND EXCURSIONS

Boracay: at White Beach boat-men offer boat tours or snorkel-ling trips. Agree itinerary and price beforehand. Bacolod and Dumaguete: tourist office arranges transport and guides for hiking trips. Dolphin- and whale-watching out of Bais: tourism office arrange boats.

## SPORTS

**Diving, windsurfing, sailing** and **cycling** are possible on Boracay. For **hiking** on Negros, contact the tourist offices.

## USEFUL CONTACTS

**Tourist Center Boracay**, Mang-gayad, Boracay Island, Aklan, tel: 036 288 3704, e-mail: info@touristcenter.com.ph www.touristcenter.com.ph Info, tel, fax and photocopy services, flight reconfirmation.

**Dept of Tourism: Regional Office VI**, Western Visayas Tourism Center, Capitol Ground, Bonifacio Drive, Iloilo City 5000, tel: 033 337 5411 or 509 3550, e-mail: deptour6@mozcom.com
**Boracay Field Office**, Balabag, Boracay, Malay, Aklan 5608, tel: 036 506 0094, fax: 036 288 3689.
**Bacolod Office**, Door no 4, Ceferina 2 Building, 22 Lacson St, Bacolod, tel: 034 709 0626.
**Bais City Tourism Office**, Bais City Hall, Bais City 6206, Ori-ental Negros, tel: 035 541 5161.
**Provincial Tourism Unit**, Ground Floor, Sikdalang Negros Building, Capitol Area, Dumaguete City, Oriental Neg-ros, tel: 035 225 1825, e-mail: negortourism@yahoo.com
**Calypso Diving**, Manggayad, Boracay Island, Aklan, tel: 036 288 3206, fax: 036 288 3478, e-mail: info@calypso-asia.com web: www.calypso-asia.com
**Boracay Foundation**: www. boracayisland.org tourism, information and bookings.
**Useful websites:**
www.tourismnegros.com
www.panay.com.ph
www.boracayonline.com
www.dumagueteinfo.com
www.oceanjet.net

| ILOILO | J | F | M | A | M | J | J | A | S | O | N | D |
|---|---|---|---|---|---|---|---|---|---|---|---|---|
| AVERAGE TEMP. °F | 79 | 79 | 81 | 84 | 84 | 82 | 81 | 81 | 81 | 82 | 81 | 81 |
| AVERAGE TEMP. °C | 26 | 26 | 27 | 29 | 29 | 28 | 27 | 27 | 27 | 28 | 27 | 27 |
| RAINFALL in | 1.6 | 1 | 1.4 | 2.2 | 4.8 | 12 | 13.4 | 14.8 | 11 | 10.4 | 7 | 3.3 |
| RAINFALL mm | 39 | 26 | 35 | 56 | 121 | 303 | 341 | 375 | 283 | 263 | 177 | 85 |
| DAYS OF RAINFALL | 8 | 6 | 5 | 5 | 10 | 19 | 20 | 19 | 19 | 18 | 14 | 11 |

PROTECT LIFE
CONSECRATE THE FAMILY
CONFESSION
COMMUNION
ADORATION
ROSARY

# 6
# Eastern Visayas

The eastern Visayas consist of Cebu, Bohol, Masbate, Leyte and Samar, the last of these being one of the Philippines' remoter and least visited areas, facing directly onto the Pacific Ocean. **Cebu** and **Bohol** are the two parts of this region best known to visitors – they are home not only to the country's third-largest city but also to some of the best beaches and the finest dive sites. As is the case with the western Visayas, the people here are friendly and getting around presents little problem, with island-hopping an enjoyable part of life.

**Cebu City**, the capital of Cebu province and site of Spain's first permanent settlement in the Philippines, is the principal gateway. The starting point for many travellers is **Mactan Island**, site of Cebu's airport and a good many luxury resorts. Quite a few small resorts lie along the coast of Cebu, while the main alternative to Mactan is **Moalboal**, a mecca for divers.

Southeast of Cebu lies Bohol, an oval island that has one of the country's best-known landscape features, the **Chocolate Hills**. Off the southwestern coast of Bohol, **Panglao Island** features some of the Visayas' best beaches and diving, the latter concentrating around the tiny island of **Balicasag**.

To the northeast, **Samar** and **Leyte** are still virgin territory for the visitor, with only two well-known sites: **Sohoton National Park**, with its beautiful limestone caves, and **Red Beach** at Palo, the World War II site where General MacArthur landed to drive the Japanese out of the Philippines.

## DON'T MISS

\*\*\* **Alona Beach:** an attractive beach with excellent diving nearby.
\*\*\* **Moalboal:** admittedly only of great interest to divers, but some of the best diving to be had in the Philippines.
\*\* **Chocolate Hills:** strange round hills filling the landscape of central Bohol.
\*\* **Sohoton National Park:** beautiful limestone caves surrounded by forest.

**Opposite:** *The front of the Basilica Minore del Santo Nino, in Cebu City, home to the Philippines' oldest Christian relic.*

**Right:** *The Taoist Temple in the exclusive Beverly Hills suburb of Cebu City is a symbol of the wealth and strength of the local Chinese community.*

### CLIMATE

Cebu has no clear-cut dry season, though most rain falls from June to October. Bohol is similar, though the rains usually come somewhat later. On Samar and Leyte there is again no clear-cut dry season, but most rain falls from November to January.

## CEBU

Cebu lies at the heart of the Visayas, consisting of a long, thin island, over 200km (125 miles) long and at most only 40km (25 miles) wide. Protected to the west by Negros and to the east by Leyte, and lying south of the typhoon belt, the area rarely suffers serious storms.

Sadly, almost all of the island's natural forest has been destroyed, but along the coast there are still numerous small offshore islands, attractive beaches and coral reefs.

### Cebu City ★

The centre of the Visayas region and the capital of Cebu province, this city of close to 700,000 people is the country's third-largest. Economically it is the Philippines' second most powerful city, with the country's largest port. The city has been a major trade centre throughout history. When Magellan arrived in 1521 the Chinese had already been here for centuries. It was not until 1565 that the Spanish came to stay, **Miguel Lopez de Legaspi** establishing Spain's first permanent settlement here.

Today, the city is expanding all the time, reaching out onto areas reclaimed from the sea. Inland, the suburbs climb up into the foothills of the central mountain range, culminating in several locations with views of the city and cool night-time temperatures.

The city itself clearly falls into old and new parts. The former, crowded and a bit down at heel, includes some of the shopping areas, including **Colon Street**, the oldest street in the Philippines and site of Legaspi's first settlement. The newer part, bustling but cleaner, spacious and clearly wealthier, is further north around Fuente Osmeña, Maxilom Avenue and the Ayala Center, the latter being a major indoor shopping centre.

Many places of interest lie in the old area, starting with the **Basilica Minore del Santo Nino** – a church that houses Cebu's most important Christian relic, a small statue of the infant Jesus that was given by Magellan in 1521 to Queen Juana, wife of Raha Humabon, the local chieftain. This basilica is the focus of Cebu's main festival, **Sinulog**, held in the third week of January.

Close to the basilica, housed in a small chapel, is **Magellan's Cross**, a replica of one planted here by Magellan when the very first Filipinos were baptized. To the southeast on the waterfront stands **Fort San Pedro**, built by the Spanish to ward off pirate attacks. Further north is the **Casa Gorordo Museum**, originally the home of Cebu's first Filipino bishop. The old house is furnished and decorated in the style of the wealthy of the late Spanish era.

In the affluent suburb of Beverly Hills, a testament to the strength of the local Chinese community, is an enormous **Taoist Temple**, well worth a visit for its insight into the Chinese Filipino world. Further out of town from here is **Tops**, a hilltop viewpoint that has spectacular views of the city below.

## MAGELLAN IN CEBU

When Ferdinand Magellan arrived in Cebu on 7 April 1521 he opened a new chapter in Philippine history. **Raha Humabon**, the local chief, was remarkably receptive to Magellan, and after making a blood pact he agreed to be baptized. This, the first baptism in the Philippines, took place on Sunday 14 April 1521. It was probably to demonstrate his fighting skills that Magellan took on Humabon's neighbour, **Lapu-Lapu**, chief of Mactan Island. On 27 April, 48 Spaniards took on 1500 of Lapu-Lapu's warriors, a clash that Magellan did not survive.

**Opposite:** *Climbing into a tricycle, the only transport available between Panagsama Beach and the nearby town of Moalboal.*
**Right:** *Shangri-La's Mactan Island Resort is probably the largest and most spectacular of the resorts strung out along the east coast of the island.*

## Mactan Island ★★

To the east of Cebu City lies Mactan Island, site of Cebu's international airport. Also here is Cebu's main tourist belt – Mactan's east coast is lined with resorts, many of them luxury developments catering to tourists from all over the world. Most of the resorts are concentrated along the intermittent beaches.

At the northern end of the island, near Punta Engaño, are two **monuments**, one to **Magellan** and the other to **Lapu-Lapu**, the local chieftain who killed Magellan on this spot in April 1521. Further south, at Maribago, are workshops dedicated to making one of Cebu's most famous traditional products – **guitars**. Visitors can buy them here, and also watch the manufacturing process.

Off Mactan's east coast lies another, quite different island – **Olango**. Though the northern half of this low-lying island is populated, with two villages, the southern half consists of a vast expanse of mangroves and mudflats that during the winter months are home to tens of thousands of migratory birds. Now a nature reserve, this is an ideal place for birdwatchers. The island is easily reached by ferry from Maribago.

## Moalboal ★★

Approximately 90km (60 miles) from Cebu City and easily reached by bus, this small, friendly town has for some years been attracting divers in large numbers. The centre of action for visitors is **Panagsama Beach**, situated about 3km (2 miles) from the town. Here, a rather untidy jumble of restaurants, guest-houses and dive operations straggles along a shore that in itself is rather disappointing for the beach lover. All the sand along this shore was swept away by a typhoon in 1984, leaving the nearest sandy beach a 15-minute boat ride to the north, at the appropriately named **White Beach**.

That Moalboal nevertheless continues to attract visitors can probably be attributed to its superb diving. Although the coral reef immediately in front of the beach was also destroyed by the 1984 typhoon (and today is slowly re-generating), other areas nearby remained intact and currently represent some of the best diving in the Visayas. The main point of interest is **Pescador Island**, a tiny slab of rock a couple of kilometres offshore and about 15 minutes by boat to the south of Panagsama Beach. The island, a marine reserve that has been extremely well protected, is the pinnacle of a submarine mountain, surrounded by a coral reef that slopes gently for a short distance before plunging off in a vertical wall into the depths of the sea. The reef top has an enormous diversity of corals, while both here and on the wall there is an abundance of marine life. A similar reef can be seen off **Tongo Point**, which is situated on the mainland about 1km (0.6 mile) south of Panagsama Beach.

Moalboal is also increasingly being used as a base to explore some of the inland areas. Hiking and mountain biking tours can be arranged at Panagsama Beach, and it is possible to make a trip to **Kawasan Falls**, an attractive place surrounded by forest vegetation, approximately 20km (12.5 miles) to the south.

## MOALBOAL DIVE SITES

Most diving here concentrates on **Pescador**, a tiny island that is the summit of a submerged mountain lying a couple of kilometres offshore. The island is ringed by a coral ledge at a depth of 3–9m (10–30ft) which becomes a sheer wall dropping to a depth of 30–50m (100–165ft). The ledge is covered with a huge wealth of corals in pristine condition, while the wall is covered in gorgonian sea fans, sponges, cup corals and many other corals. Fish life is abundant. On the western side is the 'Cathedral', an open-top funnel. A number of sites along the shore of the mainland, such as **Tongo Point**, also have reefs in excellent condition with extensive fish life.

**Above:** *The Loboc River, one of the main rivers draining Bohol, makes its way slowly through an intensely green landscape in the south of the island.*

## BOHOL

To the east of Cebu lies Bohol, tenth-largest of the Philippine islands and for the visitor one of the most attractive. The coast, with its beaches and coral reefs, is what draws most visitors, while inland lie the **Chocolate Hills**, one of the country's best-known and unique landscapes.

Historical interest lies in the large number of old Spanish churches that dot the landscape, some of the first to be built anywhere in the Philippines. They stem from a 16th-century blood pact between Legaspi and local leader Raha Sikatuna. These churches have survived despite Bohol being the scene of one of the few truly successful Filipino uprisings against the Spanish, which saw the island manage to maintain independence for 86 years (1744–1829).

### Tagbilaran and Area ★★

Tagbilaran, situated in the southwest of the island, is the capital of Bohol. It has little of interest for the visitor, though an exploration of the surrounding countryside is worthwhile. On the eastern edge of town, at **Bool**, is a memorial to the Sikatuna–Legaspi pact, while about 7km (4.5 miles) east of town is **Baclayon**, site of the Church of the Immaculate Conception, the oldest stone church in Bohol, built in 1727. Approximately 15km (10 miles) east of Tagbilaran is the town of **Loay**, the place where the River Loboc runs into the sea. From here, head inland to the village of **Loboc**, a pleasant little place on the banks of the river of the same name. This is the site of another old church, the Church of San Pedro, built a few years after the one at Baclayon. It is possible to hire boats here for trips up the river.

About 35km (20 miles) north of Tagbilaran the town of **Antequera** is known for its Sunday morning market, a

---

place to buy many of the area's handicrafts, particularly basketry. Just 1km (0.6 miles) from town are the **Mag-Aso Falls**, one of the loveliest waterfalls in Bohol.

## Chocolate Hills ★★

This strange landscape of hundreds of small rounded hills, 50–120m (165–400ft) high, lies in the middle of Bohol about 50km (30 miles) northeast of Tagbilaran, and is rated as one of the most important visitor landmarks in the country. It seems to be absolutely unique, not just to the Philippines but actually to Bohol. Although for most of the year the hills are green with grass, by the end of the dry season, in April or May, much of it has died and turned brown, giving these hills their name.

The nearest town is **Carmen**, situated at the edge of Chocolate Hills and easily accessible from Tagbilaran. Any part of the hills can be explored, but life has been made easy by the establishment of a viewpoint on the summit of one of the largest, thus ensuring an all-round view of the landscape.

The hills are said to be especially beautiful at dusk and dawn, the viewing of which entails an overnight stay in the area's limited accommodation.

> **MAKING THE CHOCOLATE HILLS**
>
> Geologists believe that the strange Chocolate Hills were created by weathering of coralline limestone lying above heavy clay. As ever, mythology has a far more colourful explanation, claiming that the hills are the debris left after a fight between two giants. The giants apparently threw rocks at each other for several days until both were quite worn out. Making friends, they left the scene of the battle, with the newly formed hills as evidence of the fight.

**Below:** *The Chocolate Hills are a landscape feature utterly unique to this one island, and are one of the Philippines' most famous sights.*

**Opposite:** *Balicasag Island, site of an important marine reserve and one of the Philippines' best dive sites.*
**Below:** *Alona Beach, Bohol's main coastal resort. On the southern shore of Panglao Island, it offers a more intimate alternative to Boracay.*

## Panglao Island ★★★

Off the southwest coast of Bohol, the island of Panglao is home to Bohol's best beaches, most notably **Alona Beach**. Here plenty of accommodation has been built among coconut groves along the edge of a stunningly beautiful white beach. Alona represents a quieter and less crowded alternative to Boracay.

Alona is good not just for the sun lover but also for the diver. Panglao is surrounded by excellent dive sites, starting with the house reef a short distance off the beach. About 9km (6 miles) to the southwest is tiny **Balicasag Island**, like Pescador Island a marine reserve with some of the country's best diving. Dive trips run daily from Alona Beach to Balicasag, or you can stay on the island. Although Balicasag has a shallow sloping coral garden, it is known mostly for its walls, where the island plunges into the depths of the sea. Here are plenty of corals and abundant fish life, including large shoals of jack, barracuda and sometimes tuna.

## Other Islands ★★

About 11km (7 miles) off the coast from Baclayon and one hour south by boat from Alona Beach lies **Pamilacan Island**, the site of a community of fishing people that used to specialize in catching whales, sharks and manta rays. Since hunting these species became illegal, and with some help in the 1990s from the World Wide Fund for Nature (WWF), these people have switched to ecotourism, using their boats and tracking skills to take visitors on whale-watching trips. Most visitors come on a day trip from the resorts on Panglao Island, though there is one small resort on Pamilacan for those who wish to stay overnight.

On the west coast of Bohol, 30km (20 miles) northwest of Tagbilaran, **Cabilao Island** is surrounded by a marine reserve known for its superb coral formations. There is accommodation, and the island can be reached from Loon on the Bohol mainland. Alternatively, dive operators in Cebu and Panglao Island often run dive trips to Cabilao.

## PANGLAO DIVE SITES

The dive sites here offer virtually every kind of diving available in the Philippines. On the northern side of Panglao Island are Napaling and Duljo, the first a beautiful, sloping coral garden with a wall, the latter a deep dive along a wall that drops to 40m (130ft). The most famous dive sites are those around nearby **Balicasag Island**, where walls and coral gardens are home to table corals, gorgonian sea fans, sponges, and large shoals of pelagic fish such as barracuda, jacks, snappers and batfish. There is also a wealth of reef fish, such as moorish idols, damselfish and butterflyfish.

## DESTRUCTIVE FISHING

Much damage has been done to coral reefs by two very destructive fishing methods: the use of **dynamite** and **cyanide**. The latter is used to catch reef fish for the aquarium trade. A small amount squirted in a crevasse on a reef stuns the fish, but kills the nearby corals. Dynamite fishing over a reef kills or stuns fish, which float to the surface, and devastates large parts of the reef. With the coral dead, fish stocks rapidly decline. Only when the reef recovers, so will fish life. Both methods are illegal, but until recently enforcement was lax. Protection has improved in most areas and many reefs are starting to recover.

**Right:** *The Leyte Landing Memorial at MacArthur Park recalls the famous scene of General Douglas MacArthur walking ashore after the successful American landings in 1944.*
**Below:** *One of the Stations of the Cross, on a hill overlooking Tacloban.*

## SAMAR AND LEYTE

These two large islands, separated by a narrow strip of water spanned by the San Juanico Bridge, form the easternmost edge of the Visayas, protecting this central part of the Philippines from the force of the Pacific Ocean. Both islands remain largely unexplored by visitors, are relatively thinly populated and still have some extensive areas of forest. Leyte, especially, has volcanic activity, with many hot springs that are now being tapped for geothermal energy.

### Tacloban and Area ★

Tacloban, the capital of Leyte, has little of interest to the visitor, though its setting is attractive – on a small bay completely enclosed by the long sweeping arm of Samar to the east. There is a great view from the hill above town, on which stands a statue of Christ.

---

### A HOWLING WILDERNESS

The American takeover of the Philippines was not without some brutality. The most famous incident occurred in **Samar** in 1901–2. A Filipino uprising in the town of Balangiga resulted in the deaths of many of the American soldiers stationed there. The reprisals were swift and extreme. General 'Jake' Smith, organizing the pacification of Samar, ordered that anyone capable of carrying arms, even 10-year-old children, were to be killed so that Samar could be turned into 'a howling wilderness'. Six months and many massacres later, he had succeeded. Smith was eventually court-martialled.

About 10km (6 miles) south of Tacloban at the town of **Palo** is **Red Beach** and **MacArthur Park**, where American troops first landed in 1944 to retake the Philippines from the Japanese. Centrepiece of the park is a dramatic memorial showing the famous scene of MacArthur and his commanders wading ashore. In Palo there is an old cathedral, while close by is **Hill 522**, scene of intense fighting between American and Japanese troops. Today, the hill has an attractive and peaceful view over the town and coast.

## Sohoton National Park ★★
Known for its deep ravines, limestone scenery and caves, this 840ha (2100-acre) national park, though situated on Samar, is most easily reached from Tacloban as a day trip. You first make for the village of Basey, where you obtain a permit and guide, and then travel for an hour by boat upriver, before entering the forest and a limestone gorge. Soon, the boat pulls up to a landing hemmed in by cliffs, and from here the guide and a ranger guide you through the most accessible cave, called Panhulugan I. Well protected by its isolation, it is still in pristine condition, with all its stalactites and stalagmites intact and free of graffiti. There are no artificial structures – all is as nature created it – and the result is stunningly beautiful.

From here it is possible to hike a little in the forest and then to continue upriver by boat, but only if the water level is high enough. Some way upriver from the cave a **natural stone bridge** spans the river gorge from one cliff face to the other, there are more caves, and at the furthest point of the park, well beyond the reach of any boat and necessitating a hike through the forest, are the 80m high (260ft) **Cabungaan Falls**.

**Below:** *Panhulugan I Cave, Sohoton National Park, Samar.*

## Eastern Visayas at a Glance

BEST TIMES TO VISIT

Cebu has no distinct dry season, though Feb–May are the driest. Apr–May are the hottest months. Bohol is similar, but rains usually arrive only in Aug. Samar and Leyte have no distinct dry season, but their rainiest period is Nov–Jan.

### GETTING THERE

Cebu's international airport is the country's second largest, with **flights** direct from Hong Kong, Japan, Malaysia and Singapore. There are many daily flights between Cebu and Manila. Tacloban is linked to Manila by regular flights. There are frequent flights into Cebu from most major Philippine cities. Regular **ferries** link Manila with the region. High-speed ferries link Tagbilaran and Cebu with Mindanao and Negros; slow ferries connect Cebu to most areas.

### GETTING AROUND

There are several **flights** a week between Cebu and Tacloban; other inter-island transport is by **ferry**. Slow ferries link most islands, while fast **catamarans** cover main routes. Regular **fast ferries** go from Cebu to Ormoc, from where there are buses to Tacloban. Fast ferries run between Cebu and Tagbilaran. Within Cebu are **buses**, some air conditioned. In Bohol, buses (like the roads) are small and battered. There are also **jeepneys**. In Samar and Leyte buses and air-conditioned

**minibuses** go from Ormoc's ferry pier to Tacloban, and jeepneys between Tacloban and Palo. Jeepney service to Basey is infrequent. Chauffeur-driven **cars** can be hired in Cebu City, Tagbilaran and Tacloban, but self-drive cars only in Cebu City. In Cebu City metered **taxis** are plentiful; to go from the city to Mactan Island drivers usually don't use the meter. For a fee they'll take you anywhere in Cebu province. In Tagbilaran and Tacloban, taxis are infrequent; most local transportation is by **tricycle**.

### WHERE TO STAY

#### Cebu City
*LUXURY*
**Cebu City Marriott Hotel**, Cardinal Rosales Avenue, Cebu City 6000, tel: 032 411 5800, web: www.marriott.com

*MID-RANGE*
**Cebu Midtown Hotel**, Fuente Osmena, Cebu City 6000, tel: 032 253 9711, e-mail: cmhsales@skyinet.net web: www.cebumidtownhotel.net

#### Mactan Island
*LUXURY*
**Shangri-La's Mactan Resort and Spa**, Punta Engano Road, Lapu-Lapu 6015, Cebu, tel: 032 231 0288, e-mail: mac@shangri-la.com web: www.shangri-la.com Comfortable rooms, two pools, gardens, beach, boats to hire, hotel's own dive operation and several restaurants.

#### Moalboal
*MID-RANGE*
**Savedra Beach Resort**, Panagsama Beach, Moalboal 6032, Cebu, tel: 032 474 0014, e-mail: info@savedrabeach resort.com web: www. savedrabeachresort.com
**Quo Vadis Beach Resort**, Panagsama Beach, Moalboal 6032, Cebu, tel: 032 474 0018, e-mail: headquovadis@aol.com web: www.moalboal.com

*BUDGET*
**Marcosas Cottages Resort**, Panagsama Beach, Moalboal 6032, Cebu, tel: 032 474 3027, e-mail: relax@ marcosas.com web: www.moalboal-cebu.com

#### Alona Beach
*MID-RANGE*
**Belleview Rock Resort**, Tawala, Panglao Island, Bohol, tel (cell): 0927 752 9850, web: www.belleviewrock.com
**Alona Tropical Beach Resort**, Alona Beach, Tawala, Panglao Island, Bohol, tel: 038 502 9024, e-mail: info@alona-tropical.com web: www.alona-tropical.com

#### Tacloban
*MID-RANGE*
**Leyte Park Resort Hotel**, Magsaysay Blvd, Tacloban, Leyte, tel: 053 325 6000, e-mail: leyteparkhotel@yahoo. com web: www.leytepark hotel.com.ph
**MacArthur Beach Resort**, Candahug, Palo, Tacloban,

Leyte, tel: 053 323 3015. Large complex laid out in gardens, next to Red Beach and MacArthur Park.

### WHERE TO EAT

At Alona Beach and Moalboal you are likely to eat at your resort. A couple of restaurants in Cebu City and Tacloban are as follows·

#### Cebu City
**Café Orchidia**, Lahug Nivel Hills, Cebu City 6000, tel: 032 233 4054. Italian and international cuisine.
**Moon Café**, Emilio Osmena Street, Guadalupe, Cebu City 6000, tel: 032 253 3635. Mexican food.

#### Tacloban
**Calle Zaragosa**, 39 Independencia St, Tacloban City 6500, Leyte, tel: 053 321 3197, e-mail: frontdesk @callezaragosa.com web: www.callezaragosa.com/calle Zcafe.html Bar food and Internet access.
**Royal Seafood Restaurant**, J. Romualdez St, Tacloban City, tel: 053 321 2120. Chinese and seafood cuisine.

### SHOPPING

In Cebu City the downtown shopping district is chaotic. Carbon Market is good for **handicrafts**, particularly **basketry**. For air-conditioned comfort head to the SM Mall or Ayala Center, a huge indoor mall with shops

selling just about everything, including handicrafts. Mactan Island has numerous **guitar** factories.

### TOURS AND EXCURSIONS

Luxury hotels on Mactan Island arrange tours for guests, while in Cebu City the tourist office, travel agents and car-hire companies can help. On Alona Beach, ask your guesthouse to arrange car, tricycle or motorbike hire. In Tacloban the tourist office will help arrange a trip to Sohoton National Park.

### SPORTS

The main sport is **diving**. **Windsurfing** is possible at some of the Mactan Island resorts. In Moalboal **mountain biking** and **hiking** trips can be arranged.

### USEFUL CONTACTS

**Department of Tourism, Regional Office VII**, G/F LDM Building, Lapu-Lapu St, Cebu City, tel: 032 254 2811 or 254 6077, airport office: 032 340 8229, e-mail: dotr7@cvis.net.ph or dot region7@gmail.com
**Regional Office VIII**, Rms

204–5, F Mendoza Commercial Complex, 141 Sto Nino St, Tacloban City, tel: 053 321 2048, e-mail: dotreg8@yahoo.com
**Savedra Dive Center**, Panagsama Beach, 6032 Moalboal, Cebu, tel: 032 474 0014, e-mail: info@savedra.com web: www.savedra.com
**Genesis Divers**, Alona Beach, 6340, Panglao Island, Bohol, tel: 038 502 9056, e-mail: dive@genesisdivers.com web: www.genesisdivers.com
**Pamilacan Island Dolphin and Whale Watching Tours**, Public Market, Poblacion, Baclayon, Bohol 6301, tel: 038 540 9279, cell: 0919 730 6108, e-mail: pamilacan@yahoo.com web: http://whales.bohol.ph
**Useful websites**: www.cebu-ph.com information on Cebu. www.supercat.com.ph high-speed ferries between Cebu and other islands. www.infomoalboal.com information on Moalboal. www.cebupacificair.com Cebu Pacific Airlines. www.bohol.ph and www.bohol-island.com information on Bohol.

| CEBU | J | F | M | A | M | J | J | A | S | O | N | D |
|---|---|---|---|---|---|---|---|---|---|---|---|---|
| AVERAGE TEMP. °F | 80 | 81 | 82 | 84 | 84 | 83 | 83 | 83 | 83 | 82 | 82 | 81 |
| AVERAGE TEMP. °C | 26 | 27 | 28 | 29 | 29 | 28 | 28 | 28 | 28 | 28 | 28 | 27 |
| RAINFALL in | 4.2 | 3 | 2.2 | 1.8 | 2.8 | 7.5 | 7.6 | 6 | 7 | 7.2 | 5.8 | 5 |
| RAINFALL mm | 104 | 75 | 54 | 44 | 71 | 188 | 192 | 148 | 174 | 182 | 148 | 127 |
| DAYS OF RAINFALL | 11 | 8 | 7 | 5 | 6 | 14 | 15 | 12 | 14 | 15 | 12 | 12 |

# 7
# Mindanao and Sulu

Recognized as the home of most of the Philippines' Muslims, much of this area has seen strife as various separatist groups struggle to create a Muslim homeland autonomous from the Manila government. Things are reasonably peaceful these days, with most of Mindanao perfectly safe to travel in. Two groups, Abu Sayyaf and the Moro Islamic Liberation Front (MILF), remain active in western Mindanao, however, while piracy is still common in and around the Sulu Islands, making these difficult areas for safe travel.

Across many parts of Mindanao, one positive result of the past violence is that fairly large tracts of wilderness, mainly rainforest, have survived more or less intact. For the energetic, hiking trails are being developed in some of the mountain areas, the most challenging climb being up **Mount Apo**, the Philippines' highest mountain.

Beaches are less well developed here than in the Visayas, but **Samal Island**, close to the city of **Davao**, is being promoted as a resort. At the northern end of Mindanao, **Camiguin Island** is already thought of as something of a tropical paradise, especially by urban Filipinos, mainly for its very friendly people and beautiful, lush scenery, complete with a climbable active volcano. In the northeast, **Siargao Island** has become a mecca for surfers.

To the southwest stretch the **Sulu Islands**, a long and scattered chain reaching out towards Borneo. Island-hopping here takes you through some of the Philippines' main Muslim areas, with a culture utterly different from most of this predominantly Christian country.

## DON'T MISS

**\*\*\* Camiguin Island:** lovely scenery and friendly people.
**\*\* Siargao Island:** surfing, fine beaches, great scenery.
**\*\* Mount Apo:** the highest mountain in the Philippines.
**\*\* Philippine Eagle Nature Center:** breeding centre for endangered Philippine eagles and other wildlife.
**\* Fort del Pilar:** home to the Marine Life Museum.
**\* Climaco Freedom Park:** views across Zamboanga.
**\* Sitangkai:** a town built on stilts over a coral reef.

**Opposite:** *A bangka on the shore of Daco, an islet offshore from Siargao Island.*

## NORTHERN MINDANAO

This region stretches from the university city of **Cagayan de Oro** in the west through **Butuan** to **Surigao** in the far north. Close to Surigao is a series of **caves**, while off the coast lies **Siargao Island**. To the southwest, Butuan is possibly one of the oldest settlements in the Philippines: prehistoric human remains have been found here, as has a large 1000-year-old ocean-going outrigger, a **balangay**, now housed in its own museum.

Inland from Cagayan de Oro one climbs into the mountains of **Bukidnon** province. Here are vast pineapple plantations, as well as the **Mount Kitanglad** range, its rainforest a known stronghold of the endangered Philippine eagle. A hiking trail leads up to Dulang-Dulang, at 2938m (9637ft) the highest peak in the range and also the second-highest mountain in the Philippines.

Off the coast between Cagayan de Oro and Butuan lies **Camiguin Island**, one of the most beautiful jewels of the entire country.

### Camiguin Island ★★★

This mountainous, 300km² (108-sq-mile) island is perhaps Mindanao's most beloved attraction. With no less than five volcanoes crammed into it, Camiguin's steep mountain slopes rise to a height of 1713m (5619ft) at Mount Mambajao, the tallest of the volcanoes. Only one of the volcanoes is presently active and that is **Hibok-Hibok**, which last erupted in 1951.

The capital of Camiguin Island is the little town of **Mambajao**. The main local activities are fishing and farming, making use of the rich volcanic soil and the nearby deep-sea trenches. The people are extremely relaxed and friendly.

**Below:** *Vast pineapple plantations spread across large areas of northern Mindanao, especially in Bukidnon province to the south of Cagayan de Oro. In the distance is the Mount Kitanglad range, an important national park.*

Beaches line much of the island's coast, though the sands are a volcanic grey. The coast is beautiful, nevertheless, made all the more so by its stupendous mountain backdrop. There is some reasonable diving here, principally on the coral reef off nearby **Mantigue Island**, on the intermittent corals around **White Island**, just offshore from

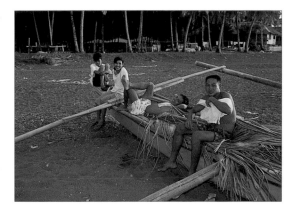

**Agoho**, on the northern tip of Camiguin, and also on the submarine slopes of **Mount Vulcan Daan**, which is one of the island's volcanoes.

Inland there are several waterfalls, as well as hot and cold springs. Close to the northern end of the island **Katibawasan Falls** is a spectacular ribbon of water plunging vertically 50m (165ft) into a pool, while not far away is **Ardent Hot Springs**. You can soak in a hot pool here, or if you are feeling energetic you can hike to the summit of Hibok-Hibok, a climb that takes about four hours from the hot spring starting point.

**Above:** *A fishing family enjoying the last rays of the setting sun on the beach at Agoho, Camiguin Island.*

### BUTUAN

Today Butuan is a rather unremarkable city that has little to attract the visitor. Yet 1000 years ago it was the trading hub of the Philippines, possibly an eastern outpost of Srivijaya, a Southeast Asian empire, and a place that had extensive contacts with China. Large finds of ancient Chinese pottery and coins have been made in Butuan, while the city is mentioned in Chinese annals of the Song and Yuan dynasties (10th–14th century). Remains of two large ocean-going vessels have been found in Butuan, one of which has been moved to Manila's National Museum.

**Right:** *Navigating a boat through the shallow reef that surrounds Guyam, a tiny islet close to Siargao Island.*
**Opposite:** *Surfing Cloud Nine on a relatively calm day. Siargao Island, especially Cloud Nine, is a surf hotspot due to its reliable and usually huge surf breaks.*

### CAMIGUIN MYTHOLOGY

According to mythology Camiguin was formed as a result of the love between a princess of northern Mindanao and a visiting warrior from the Visayas. They were forbidden to marry, but as he sailed away she attempted to swim after the boat. Sadly she drowned, but the gods took pity on her, raising her body back above the surface. Although they could not restore her to life, they could transform her into any form they wished, and so she became a paradise island and Camiguin was born. To this day, her love for the Visayan warrior remains so strong that every now and then she erupts into fiery displays of passion – the fireworks of Camiguin's volcanoes.

### Siargao Island ★★

Off the northernmost tip of Mindanao lies Siargao Island, or rather group of islands and islets. The entire island group is a protected area, due to its varied habitats, which include fragments of lowland rainforest, the country's largest mangrove swamp, beautiful coastal views and an undamaged coral reef.

A growing flow of foreign visitors has been coming to Siargao since the mid-1990s, but not because of its conservation value. This is a surf mecca. Surf breaks occur right up and down the island's east coast, though the most famous is **Cloud Nine**, just north of the town of **General Luna** (usually known simply as GL). Three-metre (9ft) waves surge in straight from the Pacific Ocean, rolling up to form almost perfect tubes before breaking on the coral reef below. The surf is best from June to November, during the typhoon season. This area is actually south of the typhoon belt and so is rarely hit by storms, but it does get the ocean swell from typhoons passing to the north.

For the non-surfer there are a number of attractions. There is quite a nice beach at GL, though the best are on some of the outer islands. **Guyam Islet**, for example, is little more than a sand bar with a few coconut palms on it, but is ringed by a white beach and has excellent snorkelling over a shallow coral reef nearby. There is another superb beach on **Daco Island**, a little further out from Guyam.

On **Bucas Grande Island**, to the southwest of Siargao but still part of the protected area, is **Suhoton Cave**, while at **Del Carmen** on the western side of Siargao boats can be hired to tour the mangroves. There are crocodiles in this swamp.

## SOUTHERN MINDANAO

The main urban area here is Davao, one of the country's largest cities. In the countryside, the landscape varies from low-lying marshland and grassy plains to the country's highest mountain, and vegetation from rice fields and plantations to dense forest. Much of the plantation farming consists of the ubiquitous coconut and banana, but you will also find the banana-like plant **abaca**, the fibres of which are spun into Manila hemp. **Durian**, the large spiny fruit that smells like a sewer and supposedly tastes like heaven, is also grown extensively in the region, its large solid trees giving the impression of forest. When in season its smell permeates even the streets of Davao, and it is no coincidence that the city is sometimes known as the durian capital of the Philippines.

### SULTAN KUDARAT

When the Spanish started to establish themselves in the Philippines they discovered that Islam had been arriving from the south. The Bruneian ruler of Manila, for example, had become a Muslim only a few years before Legaspi's arrival. Islam quickly lost ground to the Spanish in most of the country, but strongly resisted the Christian invasion in Mindanao and Sulu. In the 17th century the Spanish were repeatedly defeated by Sultan Kudarat, head of the Maguindanao Sultanate and great-great-grandson of Kabungsawan, founder of Mindanao's first Islamic sultanate.

## Davao ★

With a land area of 2440km² (880 sq miles), Davao is officially the Philippines' largest city. Most of the municipal region is open countryside and even forested mountain, however, the city itself occupying a relatively small area on the coast. Still, with a population of 900,000 it is certainly the country's second most populous city. There is little of interest within the urban area of Davao, except for the **Fuentespina Orchid Garden**, a marvellous place for lovers of flowers, and a good opportunity to see the Waling-waling, a beautiful pink or peach-coloured orchid that is Davao's emblem.

To the south of the city is the **Shrine of the Holy Infant Jesus of Prague**, set in a pleasant park and located on a hill with a good view of the city. At Lanang, on the northern side of the city, next to the Waterfront Insular Hotel is the **Davao Museum**, housing a display of artefacts belonging to some of the many tribal groups that live in Mindanao. Close by is the **T'boli Weaving Center**, where visitors can watch members of this hill group produce traditional fabrics.

About 36km (21.5 miles) northwest of the city near the town of Malagos and on the lower slopes of Mount Apo is the **Philippine Eagle Nature Center**. Run by the Philippine Eagle Foundation, the centre operates a captive breeding programme for this endangered bird. It is presently home to 36 Philippine eagles, 18 of which have been bred there. Several can be seen in huge flight cages. The centre is laid out as an attractive park that houses not just Philippine eagles but a variety of Philippine wildlife, including other endangered raptors and deer.

To date, PEF has released three captively bred eagles into the wild, though two have since died (*see* panel, page 102, for details).

Off Davao's southeast coast lies **Samal Island**, the coast of which is dotted with beaches being developed as Davao's resort. The island can be reached easily by a small but regular ferry from a wharf at Sasa, just to the north of the Waterfront Insular Hotel.

## Mount Apo ★★

At 2954m (9689ft) Mount Apo is the Philippines' highest mountain, as well as being one of the country's largest and most important national parks. This is definitely the place for nature lovers. Most of its 720km² (260 sq miles) consists of dense rainforest providing home to many rare species of plants and animals unique to this country, including the Philippine eagle.

The climb to the summit is a challenging hike, along a steep but clear trail. Most hikers start at the town of

**Above:** *Enjoying a soak in the Lake Agco hot spring.*
**Opposite:** *Davao is the largest city in Mindanao.*

### CLIMBING MOUNT APO

Most climbers start and finish their hike at Lake Agco. First you have to pass through the entrance to a geothermal plant, and from here the path climbs over a hill and then steeply downhill to the Marbel River. The path follows the river, fording it many times, before leaving it and starting the real climb. The path from here is very steep and passes through dense forest for several hours. Eventually you reach a marshy plateau, the site of Lake Venado and the overnight campsite. Set off early next morning for the two-hour hike to the summit, initially pushing through tall cogon grass and later walking over open grasslands.

**Right:** *Fishing boats sail past pile dwellings (buildings on stilts in the water) in Zamboanga.*

**FIGHTING FOR AUTONOMY**

Ever since the Spanish established a Philippine state the Muslims of the far south have fought against it. To this day the people of Sulu and southwest Mindanao have proved hostile, with guerrilla groups fighting for autonomy or independence. In 1987 the largest group, the Moro National Liberation Front, made a deal with the government that gave partial autonomy to some Muslim areas. However, a splinter group, the Moro Islamic Liberation Front, and a small, violent organization, Abu Sayyaf, continue fighting through terrorist activities, both reputedly with links to Al Qaeda.

**Kidapawan**, about two hours by bus west of Davao. From here, after collecting a permit from the municipal tourism council, located in the mayor's office, you take a jeepney to the village of **Lake Agco**, the end of the road and start of the trail. This is a beautiful spot, dense forest crowding around a steaming, bubbling volcanic lake, with a lodge and a campsite close by. Close to Lake Agco is a geothermal plant, producing electricity for Davao. The Philippines has begun exploiting its volcanic geothermal resources in a big way, and is already one of the world's main users of this energy source.

Do not attempt the climb without a guide. Engage one (and perhaps porters too) at Lake Agco and then start out early the next morning. The hike up takes 1½ days, with an overnight camp beside Lake Venado at 2400m (7872ft), and a day to return to Lake Agco. You will need to bring all your own kit, including tent and sleeping bags. Purchase your food in Davao or Kidapawan.

## THE SOUTHWEST AND SULU

Taking in the Sulu Islands and the western peninsula of Mindanao, this area is close both physically and culturally to the Malaysian province of Sabah to the west. Throughout history outsiders have found it hard to rule the area – neither the Spanish nor the Americans succeeded – and today there is much resistance to rule from Christian Manila. This is the one region that still suffers from some security problems, with two Islamic separatist groups active and even piracy not uncommon. Nevertheless, this is an extremely beautiful region, and anyone who comes here will be treated to a quite unique aspect of the Philippines.

## Zamboanga *

The capital of the southwest, Zamboanga is a largely Christian Filipino city in the midst of an otherwise Muslim region. In the city the old Spanish fort, **Fort Del Pilar**, houses the **Marine Life Museum**. Heading out of town to the northwest you come to **Pasonanca Park** and then **Climaco Freedom Park**, from where there is a good view of the city.

A few kilometres west of the city you encounter a **weaving village** run by Yakan people, one of the local ethnic groups, where fabrics made in traditional styles are manufactured and sold.

## Tawi-Tawi **

These are the most southwesterly of the Sulu Islands and closer to Sabah than they are even to Zamboanga. Here people are wholly Malay and Islamic, Malaysian Ringgit circulate freely alongside Philippine Pesos, and the rule of Manila seems to have little meaning.

The capital of this group of 300 islands is **Bongao**, situated on a small island of the same name, to the southwest of the main Tawi-Tawi Island. There is an interesting, colourful market, and close to town one can climb 314m (1030ft) Mount Bongao. Some outer islets have fine beaches which can be visited. To the southwest lies **Sibutu**, the nearest significant Philippine island to Borneo. One of the main settlements here is **Sitangkai**, a town built on stilts in shallow water above a huge coral reef. It can be reached in a day trip by boat from Bongao.

### AVOIDING TROUBLED AREAS

If travelling in western Mindanao and Sulu it is essential to follow advice on where it is and is not safe to go. Although the degree and locations of trouble vary, the main trouble spots in Mindanao are the Cotabato and Maguindanao provinces, where the MILF remains strong, and Zamboanga province where Abu Sayyaf carries out occasional terrorist acts and kidnappings. Abu Sayyaf is also very active in Basilan and parts of Sulu. Piracy is not uncommon throughout Sulu. If a local tells you that a certain locality is a no-go area, they mean it.

### SULU AND THE CHINESE

Sulu is believed to have traded with China as far back as the 8th century, and to have had extensive dealings during the Song and Yuan dynasties (10th–14th centuries). Sulu exports to China included lacquer, beeswax, tortoise shells and pearls, the latter often as big as 2.5cm (1 in) across. Sulu sent several envoys to China, and when China's foreign trade became state-controlled during the early part of the Ming dynasty (early 15th century), Sulu was a port of call for the first of the great imperial voyages made under the command of Zheng He.

# Mindanao and Sulu at a Glance

Due to the complex effects of the northeast and southwest monsoons, the best times to visit vary quite considerably in different parts of Mindanao. Davao has a remarkably low rainfall, which remains steady throughout the year. Mount Apo is basically the same, though being a mountain it receives considerably more rain than Davao. Hikers should be prepared for rain at any time. Climbing the mountain is extremely popular during Holy Week, the week preceding Easter, so this would be a good time to avoid. Northern Mindanao receives most of its rain between November and January, and although there is no clearly defined dry season **Mar–May** are the driest months. The typhoon season (Jun–Nov) is the best time for surfers to be on Siargao. Camiguin has its annual Lanzones Festival in October, celebrating the harvest of this fruit, which is grown extensively there. The southwest has a short dry season in March and April; the highest rainfall occurs in Oct–Nov.

Daily **flights** and regular **ferries** connect Manila with Davao, Cagayan de Oro and Zamboanga. There are daily flights from Zamboanga to the Sulu Islands. Ferries ply this route but may not be entirely safe. Regular ferries link Benoni, Camiguin Island's

main port, with Balingoan, the nearest mainland harbour. There are sometimes flights between Cebu and Camiguin, but the schedule is unreliable. For Siargao, there are two flights a week from Cebu, while nearby Surigao is served by five flights a week from Cebu and daily flights from Manila. A daily ferry runs from Surigao to Siargao's port, Dapa.

**Jeepneys** and **taxis** are plentiful in Davao, Cagayan de Oro and Zamboanga. In Surigao transport is by **motorized tricycles**. To reach Mount Apo from Davao, air-conditioned and ordinary **buses** run frequently to Kidapawan, from where a jeepney can be taken to Lake Agco. To travel between the different parts of Mindanao, frequent air-conditioned and ordinary buses ply all the main routes. In addition, there are **flights** between Davao and Zamboanga, and between Davao and Cagayan de Oro. On Camiguin and Siargao, use a jeepney or hired **motorbike**. In the Sulu Islands everyone uses a **boat**, either scheduled ferries or by special hire.

### Davao
#### LUXURY
**Marco Polo Davao Hotel**, CM Recto St, Davao City 8000, tel: 082 221 0888, fax: 082 225 0111, e-mail: davao@marcopolohotels.com

web: www.marcopolohotels.com Luxury international hotel in a convenietnt downtown location.

#### MID-RANGE
**Apo View Hotel**, J Camus Street, Davao City 8000, tel: 082 221 6430, e-mail: info@apoview.com web: www.apoview.com
**Regency Inn**, Villa Abrille St, Davao City 8000, tel: 082 227 7777, e-mail: regency@regencyinndavao.com web: www.regencyinndavao.com

### Camiguin Island
#### MID-RANGE
**Paras Beach Resort**, Yumbing, Mambajao, Camiguin Island, tel: 088 387 9008, web: www.parasbeachresort.com At northern tip of island; air-conditioned rooms; restaurant; pool; diving facilities.

#### BUDGET
**Caves Resort**, Agoho, Mambajao, Camiguin Island, tel/fax: 088 387 0077, e-mail: cavesresort@yahoo.com web: www.cavesdiveresort camiguin.com Beachside resort; rooms built up to the edge of the beach; cottages built in a coconut palm grove.

### Siargao Island
#### MID-RANGE
**Sagana Resort**, Cloud Nine, General Luna, Siargao Island, Surigao del Norte, tel (cell): 0919 809 5769, e-mail: sagana@cloud9surf.com web: www.cloud9surf.com

## Mindanao and Sulu at a Glance

### Zamboanga
#### LUXURY
**Garden Orchid Hotel**,
Governor Camins Ave,
Zamboanga City 7000, tel:
062 991 0031, fax: 062 991
0035, e-mail: info@garden
orchidhotel.com web:
www.gardenorchidhotel.com
A top-class city hotel.

### Davao
**Top of the Apo**, Apo View
Hotel, J Camus St, Davao City,
tel: 082 221 6430. Interna-
tional cuisine; view of the city.
**La Parilla**, Waterfront Insular
Hotel, Lanang, Davao City
8000, tel: 082 233 2881.
Seafood restaurant.

### Zamboanga
**Alavar Seafood Restaurant**,
Don Alfaro St, Tetuan,
Zamboanga City 7000, tel:
062 991 2483, e-mail: sales@
alvarrestaurant.com web:
www.alvarrestaurant.com
Excellent seafood.

The **Department of Tourism**
in Davao can help arrange a
tour of the southern Mindanao
region, which includes making arrangements for a hike up
Mount Apo. The **Kidapawan
Municipal Tourism Council** is
also of great help. Indeed,
anyone intending to climb
Mount Apo via the Lake Agco
route must first obtain a permit here. There are car hire
companies in Davao, but only
with chauffeur-driven cars: as

with the Visayas, self-drive car
hire is not an option. The
**Department of Tourism** in
Zamboanga may be able to
help with travel plans in the
Sulu Islands, but for trips to
Camiguin and Siargao Islands
you will need to make your
own arrangements.

**Diving** facilities are still rather
limited in Mindanao. How-
ever, dive operations have
been set up on Samal and
Siargao Islands, while on
Camiguin Island a couple of
resorts have facilities. **Hiking** is
well established on Mount
Apo, and local **mountaineer-
ing** groups have set up trails
on more of Mindanao's moun
tains. The Department of
Tourism in Cagayan de Oro
may be able to help with
arrangements to climb Mount
Kitanglad. Davao has three
**golf** courses. Two of them are
full 18-hole courses and one is
a nine-hole course. Surfboards
can be hired at most resorts on
Siargao. The island is also
known for deep-sea angling.

**Department of Tourism,
Regional Office IX**, Lantaka

Hotel By the Sea, Valderrosa
St, Zamboanga City 7000,
tel: 062 992 6242, e-mail:
dotr9@yahoo.com
**Regional Office X**, A Velez
Street, Cagayan de Oro City
9000, tel: 088 726 394 or
723 696, e-mail: dotr10@
yahoo.com
**Regional Office XI**, 5/F,
Landco Corporate Center
Building, JP Laurel Ave,
Davao City 8000, tel:
082 225 1940, e-mail:
dotr11@yahoo.com
**Region XII**, 2/F Hua Hing
Building, 17 Sinsuat Avenue,
Cotabato City 9600, tel:
064 421 1110, e-mail:
dotregion12@yahoo.com
**Region XIII**, G/F Grateful
Realty Corp Building, 008 Pili
Drive, Butuan City 8600, tel:
085 341 8413, e-mail:
dotr13@yahoo.com
**Useful websites**:
www.islandcamiguin.com
(information on Camiguin).
www.davaocity.gov.ph
www.clickdavao.com
www.discoverdavao.com
(information on Davao).
www.discoversiargao.com
www.siargao.com (informa-
tion on Siargao Island).
www.flyseair.com (Southeast
Asia Airlines).

| DAVAO | J | F | M | A | M | J | J | A | S | O | N | D |
|---|---|---|---|---|---|---|---|---|---|---|---|---|
| AVERAGE TEMP. °F | 81 | 81 | 81 | 82 | 82 | 82 | 81 | 81 | 81 | 82 | 82 | 81 |
| AVERAGE TEMP. °C | 27 | 27 | 27 | 28 | 28 | 28 | 27 | 27 | 27 | 28 | 28 | 27 |
| RAINFALL in | 4.7 | 4.2 | 3.3 | 5.7 | 17.4 | 7.5 | 6 | 6.8 | 7.2 | 6.8 | 5.2 | 3.8 |
| RAINFALL mm | 119 | 107 | 85 | 145 | 189 | 189 | 154 | 175 | 181 | 174 | 131 | 98 |
| DAYS OF RAINFALL | 13 | 12 | 11 | 11 | 16 | 18 | 15 | 14 | 15 | 15 | 14 | 13 |

# 8
# Palawan

The third-largest of the Philippine islands, this long sliver of land has been dubbed the country's last frontier. Its 14,650km² (5656 sq miles), comprising 1768 islands, are home to only 900,000 people, and despite rapid population growth the region is still rich in tracts of forest. Wildlife abounds, including numerous species of bird and mammal that live nowhere else. So important is Palawan to Southeast Asian conservation that in 1990 UNESCO declared the whole of Palawan a Man and the Biosphere Reserve.

Visitors come to Palawan almost solely for its natural beauty. Protected areas are high on the list of places to visit, as are some of the many hundreds of islands, where resorts offer the chance to play at Robinson Crusoe.

The northern parts of Palawan are most easily reached by plane from Manila. The most famous of these places are **Bacuit Bay** and the little town of **El Nido**, site of a cluster of limestone islands complete with towering peaks and dizzying cliffs. Further north the **Calamian** group of islands includes **Coron Island**, where the highly endangered Philippine cockatoo can still be seen, **Coron Bay**, which is rapidly becoming a new mecca for wreck diving, and **Calauit Island**, a wildlife sanctuary that has become a natural home to several species of African mammals.

Further south, **St Paul's Underground River National Park** is reachable from provincial capital **Puerto Princesa**. Most isolated of all, **Tubbataha Reef**, a major attraction to divers, is a nine-hour boat journey from the city.

## DON'T MISS

★★★ **El Nido:** sheer cliffs and isolated beaches.
★★★ **St Paul's Underground River National Park:** a river flowing in a limestone cave.
★★★ **Sabang:** fantastic beach.
★★★ **Calauit Island:** a safari with African wildlife.
★★★ **Tubbataha Reef:** exciting underwater life.
★★ **Palawan Wildlife Rescue and Conservation Center:** get really close to crocodiles.
★★ **Coron Island:** visit the stunning inland lake.
★★ **Coron Bay:** one of Asia's best wreck diving sites.

**Opposite:** *Cottages of the Miniloc Island Resort, Miniloc Island, El Nido.*

**Above:** *A small river lined with mangroves cuts through the shore at the eastern end of Sabang Beach, demarcating the edge of the forest in St Paul's Underground River National Park.*

## CENTRAL PALAWAN

This is the narrow waist of the province, where in places the island is barely 10km (6 miles) wide. It is the most populated and developed part of Palawan, and the home of Puerto Princesa, the provincial capital. Though this area has more cleared land than almost anywhere else in Palawan, there is still much rugged, forested terrain, notably **Cleopatra's Needle**, at 1593m (5225ft) the highest mountain in central Palawan, as well as the highly protected area of St Paul's Underground River National Park. Between Puerto Princesa City and St Paul's is island-studded **Honda Bay**, a pretty area with a few beaches and some good snorkelling that can be visited by boat from the city.

### Puerto Princesa *

Established in 1970, the municipality of Puerto Princesa is huge, covering much of central Palawan, and making it the second-largest municipal area in the Philippines, after Davao. The total population, however, is only 157,000, and the city itself is quite small, if rather sprawling. It has a reputation as the cleanest city in the Philippines, the result of rigorously enforced laws introduced by the environmentally conscious city government. Even the tricycles have ashtrays!

The heart of the city is Rizal Avenue, running east–west for 3km (2 miles) from near the port to the airport. Most of the city's main buildings are laid out along or near this road, including the market, shops, banks, museum, government buildings and many of the hotels.

There are few specific sights within the city, apart from the **Palawan Museum**, situated next to Mendoza Park. As can be expected, it chronicles the history and describes the people of Palawan. Just outside the urban area, at Irawan, a few kilometres north of the city, is the **Palawan Wildlife Rescue and Conservation Center**, a place that aims through research to conserve the two species of Philippine crocodiles. The institute houses a large number of crocodiles and is also home to a small collection of other species of Palawan wildlife, the result of illegally caught animals confiscated by police. Beyond Irawan, continuing along the road towards Aborlan to the south of Puerto Princesa, is the **Iwahig Prison and Penal Colony**. Not exactly the kind of place one would normally visit, Iwahig is a prison without bars, where the convicts work in the open fields. Handicrafts made by the convicts can even be bought at the prison's own handicraft store.

### CROCODILES

The **Palawan Wildlife Rescue and Conservation Center**, just outside Puerto Princesa, was set up with Japanese funding to find ways to protect the Philippines' two species of crocodile, the saltwater and Philippine crocodiles. Research has gone into environmental conservation, farming techniques and ways to improve the animals' rather negative image with the public. Work is ongoing, and visitors are able to undertake free tours of some of the breeding pens, as well as a natural habitat containing a number of crocodiles.

**Left:** *Visitors viewing crocodiles captively bred at the Palawan Wildlife Rescue and Conservation Center, Puerto Princesa.*

## Sabang and St Paul's Underground River ★★★

Approximately 80km (50 miles) north of the urban area of Puerto Princesa, but still within the municipality, lies central Palawan's principal visitor attraction, St Paul's Underground River National Park. Awarded World Heritage Site status in 1999, the park consists of a river that runs for 8km (5 miles) through a limestone cave before opening into a lagoon that is separated from the sea only by a low sandbar. The whole area is surrounded by protected rainforest, above which stands the 1028m (3372ft) dome-shaped peak of Mount St Paul's, named in the 19th century by British sailors for its apparent resemblance to St Paul's Cathedral in London.

Access from Puerto Princesa is by a rough road to **Sabang**, a tiny village with one of Palawan's most magnificent beaches. It is worth making a trip to Sabang for the beach alone. At Sabang, you can either walk to the national park along the beach and then through rainforest, a distance of about 4km (2.5 miles), or hire a boat for the 15-minute ride. Entry permits are essential, available either at the national park office in Puerto Princesa, or at the small office in Sabang.

The boat ride takes you to a beach from where it is a 200m (219yd) walk through forest to the check-in desk, where permits are checked and boats arranged. Small outrigger boats equipped with powerful lamps take visitors into the underground river, upstream for 1km (0.6

**Below:** *A guided tour along St Paul's Underground River.*

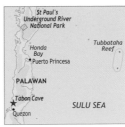

**Left:** *A group of Moorish idols swim past a soft coral clinging to a rocky wall, close to Bird Island, in the north of Tubbataha Reef National Marine Park.*

mile) to the inner end of the 'Highway', a long and perfectly straight stretch of high-roofed tunnel, before turning around and returning. Many areas have fascinating stalactites and stalagmites, and one is constantly surrounded by the twitching noises of thousands of bats and swiftlets.

Outside the cave the forest teems with wildlife, especially Philippine macaques and monitor lizards, and is worth exploring. Around the picnic area close to the beach, Tabon birds can frequently be seen. This highly endangered flightless bird thrives at St Paul's. One of its unique features is the enormous mound of sand that it builds over its eggs.

## TUBBATAHA REEF

Lying 150km (95 miles) southeast of Puerto Princesa, this 33,200ha (120-sq-mile) reef is a national marine park with a huge diversity of coral and fish living on and around it. Consisting of two atolls, each with their own small islands, the reef is also breeding ground for several species of maritime bird, especially boobies and noddies.

The reef is a diver's paradise, with virtually everything known to exist in the seas around the Philippines available here, from the tiniest corals and reef fish to sharks, turtles and manta rays. Its isolation and usually rough seas have helped protect it, and the only access is via live-aboard dive cruises that visit this area during the March–May calm season. These dive ships usually operate out of either Puerto Princesa or Iloilo.

### THE IMPORTANCE OF TUBBATAHA REEF

Tubbataha consists of two coral atolls, each with a small islet surrounded by extensive reefs, and separated by a channel 8km (5 miles) wide. The nearest human settlement is a seaweed farm on Arena Reef, about 80km (50 miles) to the northeast. Traditionally, the reef has been protected from human interference for nine months of the year by rough seas, but over the past decade **dynamite** fishing has been conducted through much of the year. Protection of the reef is essential not only for its own beauty but also because it is believed to supply a very large proportion of the fish fry that eventually migrate all round Palawan, sustaining the entire province's fishing industry.

**Right:** *A fishing village adjacent to the town of Taytay, seen from the walls of an old Spanish fort. Situated in the north of Palawan, Taytay was once the provincial capital. Today, it is a rather remote, sleepy town.*

## NORTHERN PALAWAN

This is one of the remotest regions of the Philippines. Much of it remains densely forested, though many areas are being rapidly cleared as settlers move in. The roads are rough and public transport unreliable. Boats are often the best way to get around, and the whole region is generally better accessed from Manila, via the airport at **El Nido**, than by road from Puerto Princesa.

In the south, places of interest include the small beach resort of **Port Barton** on the west coast, while close to the town of Roxas on the east coast is the resort island of **Coco-Loco**. To the north is the town of **Taytay**, which is the access point for the **Club Noah Isabelle** resort, while further north still lies **El Nido**, one of the gems of the Philippines.

### Taytay ★

Taytay, once the capital of Palawan, lies on the northeast coast about 150km (95 miles) north of Puerto Princesa. The town itself is a quiet little place, its only specific site of interest being the ruins of an 18th-century Spanish **fort** built beside the harbour. The ruined walls were made from local coral. Offshore are numerous islands, which can be reached by hiring a boat at Taytay. Some of the islands have small resorts, most importantly **Apulit Island**, site of Club Noah Isabelle, an exclusive resort that claims to have a strong commitment to sustainable ecotourism. West of Taytay is **Malampaya Sound**, a vast enclosed bay that connects with Palawan's west coast. Malampaya Sound is so rich in marine life that it has become one of the Philippines' major fishing and fish farming grounds.

### El Nido and Bacuit Bay ★★★

Situated 50km (30 miles) north of Taytay, this is one of the most beautiful spots in the Philippines. The bay contains a large number of islands, most characterized by towering limestone cliffs that are essentially a marine version of the famous karst limestone peaks of southern China. Some of the shorelines are marked by stunning beaches, while many of the less precipitous island slopes are covered with fragments of rainforest, home to hornbills, monkeys and monitor lizards.

**El Nido town** lies at the northern end of the area, itself in a dramatic setting, located on a sweeping sandy bay backed by sheer cliffs. It is a small place with hardly any traffic, apart from a few jeepneys that link the town to Taytay and Puerto Princesa. El Nido town has plenty of accommodation and numerous restaurants, with several more resorts spread out along the coast further south at Corong-Corong.

**ETHNIC GROUPS**

The great majority of Palawan's inhabitants are immigrants from other parts of the Philippines, especially the Visayas. Inward migration is causing the population to grow by 4% annually, greatly threatening the natural environment. The original inhabitants, now very much a minority in their own land, are the Tagbanua, the Pala'wan, Batak, Tau't Batu and Jama Mapun. Some of these are being assimilated into Filipino society, but others still live a primitive existence in the forests. Another minority group, though immigrants from Sulu, are the Badjao – the Sea Gypsies – who spend their entire lives on the water.

**Left:** *Vertical limestone cliffs tower above the township of El Nido, principal settlement in Bacuit Bay. Situated in a very remote area of north-western Palawan, the immense beauty of the island-studded bay was only discovered by the outside world in the early 1990s. Now, with its own small airport and daily flights to and from Manila, El Nido is a must-see beauty spot.*

El Nido town is a pleasant place to relax, but the main attraction has to be the islands. Boats can be hired to make leisurely tours around almost any of the islands (a couple are closed due to the presence of the military), or simply to ferry you to and from a beach of your choice. The boatmen all know the best spots. There are a number of good snorkelling sites, and for divers there are several dive operators based in El Nido town. Unfortunately, although the snorkelling is very good, with excellent corals occurring in the shallow waters, at greater depths dynamite fishing has caused extensive damage, and good corals exist only in patches. Nevertheless, there is plenty of interesting marine life; turtles, for example, can be seen frequently.

One of the most interesting islands for a tour is **Miniloc**, where two lagoons, both ringed by sheer lime-stone cliffs, can be explored. Here the scenery is stunning and the water crystal clear. Turtles frequently use these sheltered waters, and there have even been occasional reports of whales entering the larger lagoon. Close to Miniloc is one of the symbols of El Nido – the **Tres Marias**, an islet consisting of three jagged slabs of rock pointing upwards from the water's surface. It is immedi-ately around this islet that some of the best snorkelling can be found.

For those who want to experience island life at close quarters, several islands have resorts, most notably Malapacao, Langen and Miniloc islands. The last

**Below:** *Miniloc Island Resort, nestling in its own cove and surrounded by sheer limestone cliffs.*

two have truly luxu-rious resorts owned by a company called Ten Knots. The one set on **Langen Island**, called (strangely enough) Lagen Island Resort, is flanked by enormous cliffs and set against dense for-est that is well worth exploring.

## CALAMIAN ISLANDS

The Calamian Islands are the most northerly part of Palawan, and consist mainly of Busuanga, Coron, Culion and Calauit islands. The main town and focus for visitors is **Coron**, situated confusingly on Busuanga Island.

Unlike most of Palawan, many of the islands, with the exception of Coron Island, have been deforested, and have at best patches of scrub. A large part of Busuanga Island is given over to what is claimed to be Asia's largest cattle ranch.

### Coron Town and Coron Bay ★★

Coron town is a small, friendly place that stretches along the shoreline at the eastern end of Coron Bay. Behind the town rises **Mount Dapias**, topped with a satellite television receiver. It is well worth climbing this hill for its superb view across the bay and **Coron Island**. Just to the east of town is **Makinit Hot Spring**, consisting of a pleasant hot pool close to the shore. It can be reached by taking a tricycle to the end of the road and then walking for about 20 minutes along the shore.

**Above:** *View from Mount Dapias across Coron Bay to the cliffs of Coron Island.*

### PALAWAN WILDLIFE

Although Palawan's wildlife is similar to that of Borneo, there are species unique to this island. These include the Palawan peacock pheasant, and Palawan hornbill. Both are highly endangered despite the survival of the forest. Other animals found in both Palawan and Borneo include the scaly anteater, Asian short-clawed otter, mouse deer and porcupine. The waters around Palawan are home to endangered species such as the hawksbill, green and Olive Ridley turtles, and the dugong, or sea cow.

**Above:** *A Japanese wartime wreck in Coron Bay, Calamian Islands.*

### JAPANESE WRECKS

Coron Bay is littered with the wrecks of Japanese ships sunk by US aircraft in 1944. To date 12 wrecks have been found, some of which are now regularly dived. All are about a two-hour boat ride from Coron town, located in the western part of the bay. They include the *Okikawa Maru*, a 10,000-tonne tanker in 26m (85ft) of water; the *Akitsushima*, a warship lying 38m (125ft) down; and the *Olympia Maru* and *Kogyo Maru*, both freighters lying on their side 25m (80ft) and 34m (110ft) down respectively. Most have extensive coral growth, and are home to a lot of fish, including lionfish and the dangerous scorpionfish.

Many houses in Coron are built on stilts over the water. This is especially true on the eastern edge of town where a whole village of **Badjao** fisherfolk live. The result, though picturesque, has rendered this part of Coron Bay far from pristine. Swimming close to the town is definitely not recommended!

Coron town is the local headquarters for several diving operations, as the area is slowly becoming a major wreck diving centre. The wrecks are the result of a World War II air raid by US aircraft on a fleet of Japanese supply ships that had hidden among the islands of Coron Bay. Various ships have been identified and surveyed, mostly around **Tangat Island**, about two hours by boat west of Coron town. Many of the wrecks are still surprisingly intact, with their cargoes clearly visible. Marine life around them is extensive, corals growing well on the hulls and fish making good use of the many nooks and crannies. Being a largely enclosed bay, underwater visibility is bad, but for those interested in wrecks this is one of the best sites in Southeast Asia.

### Coron Island ★★

To the south of Coron town lies Coron Island, a place of jagged limestone peaks, rather like El Nido but forming one solid land mass. It is a mysterious place, whose inhabitants, members of the Tagbanua ethnic group, have gone to some pains to protect their environment and keep outsiders away. As a result, the less rocky areas are covered with rainforest, where the endangered Philippine cockatoo can still be seen. The entire island has been declared a protected area.

The island also has numerous freshwater lakes, which are sacred to the Tagbanua. Only one is accessible: **Lake Kayangan**, situated on the northwestern side of the island. A boat trip from Coron town will take you to a lagoon on the west coast, from where it is a short hike to the lake. The eastern side of the island, facing the open sea and site of the Tagbanua's two villages, is out of bounds due to the islanders' reluctance to accept visitors.

**Left:** *A view across the town of Coron and the sheltered waters of Coron Bay.*

### A HOME FOR AFRICAN WILDLIFE

In 1977, 104 animals, representing eight species of African wildlife, were taken from Kenya and put on isolated **Calauit Island**. Those species were bushbuck, eland, gazelle, giraffe, impala, topi, waterbuck and zebra. Since then the gazelles and topi have died out. The others, however, have flourished, the total herd now standing at about 500 animals. The animals' grazing and browsing habits have converted the island's scrubby environment into a savannah of grass and scattered trees, and anyone watching the herds moving across this landscape could easily believe that they had been transported to Africa. Native species have also fared well, especially the highly endangered Calamian Deer, of which there are over 1000 on Calauit.

## Calauit Island ★★★

At the far northwestern end of Busuanga Island lies Calauit Island, separated from its larger neighbour only by a large mangrove swamp. Back in 1976, as the last stronghold of the Calamian deer, a locally endemic animal, the island was designated a wildlife sanctuary. In 1977, then-president and dictator Marcos ordered all the island's inhabitants to move out, replacing them with eight species of African mammals and thereby creating one of Asia's most remarkable safari parks.

Today, despite attempts by the former inhabitants to return, the sanctuary still exists and most of the African mammals and Philippine wildlife are thriving. In those extensive areas where the African animals are allowed to roam at will they have moulded the landscape into a savannah. Herds of giraffe, zebra, impala, waterbuck and eland can easily be seen, along with large numbers of the resurgent Calamian deer and many birds.

**Left:** *A herd of eland, a species of African antelope, wanders through savannah-like grassland in Calauit Island Wildlife Sanctuary, off the northwestern tip of Busuanga Island.*

# Palawan at a Glance

### BEST TIMES TO VISIT

Palawan is hot and humid all year, and from mid-May to the end of December is rainy too. Unpaved roads turn to mud and become impassable. The only dry period is **January** to early **May**, when roads are dry and dusty but usable.

### GETTING THERE

Puerto Princesa is reached by direct daily flights from Manila and three times weekly from Cebu. From other centres it can be reached via Manila or Cebu. Northern Palawan is reached by daily flights from Manila to El Nido. Calamian Islands are served by daily flights from Manila to Busu-anga Airport. Tubbataha Reef is accessible only by **cruise boat** from Puerto Princesa or Iloilo. **Ferries** connect Puerto Princesa with Manila, Iloilo, Bacolod and Cebu, and Coron with Manila and Batangas.

### GETTING AROUND

**Jeepneys** link Sabang with Puerto Princesa daily. **Buses** leave Puerto Princesa every morning to go to Roxas and Taytay. Up to four buses run daily between Puerto Princesa and El Nido. During summer (April–May) a **ferry** links Sabang and El Nido twice a week. Calauit Island can be reached from Coron town by one daily bus, which goes to the nearby town of Quezon. From here **boats** can be hired to cross the channel to the island. Alternatively,

boats can be hired for the entire journey between Coron town and Calauit, taking about six hours one way.

### WHERE TO STAY

**Puerto Princesa**
*LUXURY*
**Hotel Fleuris Palawan**, Lacao St, Puerto Princesa 5300, tel: 048 434 4338, e-mail: info@ fleuris.com www.fleuris.com
*MID-RANGE*
**The Legend Palawan Hotel**, Malvar St, Puerto Princesa 5300, Palawan, tel: 048 434 4270, e-mail: customercare@ legendpalawan.com.ph web: www.legendpalawan.com.ph
*BUDGET*
**Badjao Inn**, 350 Rizal Ave, Puerto Princesa 5300, tel: 048 433 2761, e-mail: badjao_inn@yahoo.com Pleasant; around a quadrangle with a garden and restaurant.
**Puerto Pension**, 35 Malvar St, Puerto Princesa 5300, Palawan, tel: 048 433 2969, e-mail: ppension@pldtdsl.net web: www.pal-onl.com/pension

**Taytay**
*LUXURY*
**Amanpulo Resort**, Pamalican Island, Cuyo Islands, Palawan, Manila booking off: PO 456, Pasay Tramo Post Office, Pasay City 1300, Metro Manila, tel: 02 759 4040, e-mail: amanpulo@amanresorts.com web: www.amanpulo.com
The height of luxury on its own private island in the Sulu Sea. Perhaps the most exclusive resort in the Philippines.

*BUDGET*
**Casa Rosa Inn and Pizza Bar**, Taytay, tel (cell): 0918 388 1063. Bungalows set in a hill-top garden, with views of the fort and harbour.

**El Nido**
*LUXURY*
**Lagen Island Resort**, El Nido. Manila office: Ten Knots Development Corporation, 18/F, 8747 Paseo de Roxas, Salcedo Village, Makati City 1226, Metro Manilla, tel: 02 894 5644, e-mail: holiday @elnidoresorts.com www. elnidoresorts.com Modern, luxurious resort in an island setting with beach and forest.
*MID-RANGE*
**Dolarog Beach Resort**, Dolarog, El Nido 5313, e-mail: info@dolarog.com web: www.dolarog.com
A self-contained resort on coast south of El Nido town.
**Lally and Abet Beach Resort**, El Nido, tel (cell): 0920 905 6822; Manila contact tel: 02 928 1299, e-mail: info@lally andabet.com web: www. lallyandabet.com Bungalows beside beach, with own restaurant, on edge of El Nido town.

**Calamian Islands**
*LUXURY*
**Club Paradise**, Dimakya Island, Coron. Manila office: Regent Bldg, Malunggay Rd, FTI Complex, Taguig, Manila 1630, tel (Manila): 02 838 4956, e-mail: reservations@ clubparadisepalawan.com www.clubparadisepalawan.

com On its own island off the north coast of Busuanga.

***BUDGET***
**Sea Dive Resort**, Coron, Palawan 5316, tel (cell): 0920 945 8714, e-mail: seadive@ seadiveresort.com web: www. seadiveresort.com Built on piles out over the water; restaurant; dive operations.

### WHERE TO EAT

*Puerto Princesa*
**Kalui Restaurant**, 369 Rizal Ave, Puerto Princesa 5300, tel: 048 433 2580. Filipino seafood.

*El Nido*
**Shipwrecked Bar and Restaurant**, Serena St, Buena Suerte, El Nido, tel (cell): 0916 293 3281. Asian and European dishes.

### TOURS AND EXCURSIONS

Getting around Palawan can be difficult, time-consuming and tiring. Several travel agencies can arrange some or all of your transport. Most are based in Puerto Princesa, though they may have branches in Coron and El Nido, and some have offices in Manila too.

### SPORT

The most important sport for visitors to Palawan is **diving**. Although some reefs have been damaged by dynamite and cyanide fishing, many are still in pristine condition. Dive operations are based in Puerto Princesa, El Nido,

Coron town and Club Paradise. Organize trips upon arrival or in Manila, using one of several dive specialists. Arrange live-aboard cruises to Tubbataha Reef in advance through a Manila dive specialist as places are limited. **Yacht** charter and **kayaking** are possible in Coron town. **Trekking** can be arranged (e.g. to climb Cleopatra's Needle). Always take a guide. Make arrangements through a travel agent in Puerto Princesa.

### USEFUL CONTACTS

**Department of Tourism, Regional Office IV**, Rm 208, DOT Building, TM Kalaw St, Ermita, Manila 1000, tel: 02 524 1969 or 542 1528, e-mail: lcjurilla@tourism.gov.ph
**El Nido Municipal Tourism Office**, El Nido, Palawan, tel (cell): 0926 993 8803, e-mail: info@elnidotourism.com web: www.elnidotourism.com
**WG & A Superferry**, Aboitiz Transport Systems Corporation, 42 Rizal Ave, Puerto Princesa 5300, tel: 048 434 5736, web: www.superferry.com.ph
**Airphilexpress**, R1 Hangar, APC Gate 1, Andrews Ave,

Nichols, Pasay City, Metro Manila 1300, tel: 02 855 9000, e-mail: info@air philippines.com.ph web: www.airphilexpress.com Flights from Manila to Puerto Princesa and Busuanga.
**Zest Air**, tel (Manila): 02 888 2002, tel (Puerto Princesa): 048 433 5541, e-mail: customerrelations@zestair. com.ph web: www.zestair. com.ph Flights from Manila to Puerto Princesa and Busuanga.
**Sea Dive Center**, Coron, Palawan 5316, tel (cell): 0920 945 8714, e-mail: seadive@ seadiveresort.com web: www.seadiveresort.com Dive operator in Coron town, specializing in wreck diving in Coron Bay.
**Websites:** www.visitpuerto princesa.com
www.elnidopalawan.com
www.alltravelpalawan.com
www.palawaninfo.com
www.palawantrips.com
(info on Palawan);
www.palawan.com Palawan hotel information.
www.pcsd.ph The Palawan Council for Sustainable Development, with information about Palawan's protected areas.

| PUERTO PRINCESA | J | F | M | A | M | J | J | A | S | O | N | D |
|---|---|---|---|---|---|---|---|---|---|---|---|---|
| AVERAGE TEMP. °F | 81 | 81 | 81 | 82 | 82 | 82 | 81 | 81 | 81 | 81 | 81 | 81 |
| AVERAGE TEMP. °C | 27 | 27 | 27 | 29 | 29 | 28 | 27 | 27 | 27 | 27 | 27 | 27 |
| RAINFALL in | 1 | 0.6 | 0.9 | 1.4 | 5.2 | 7 | 7 | 6.6 | 7.3 | 8.2 | 8.1 | 4.6 |
| RAINFALL mm | 27 | 15 | 23 | 36 | 131 | 177 | 176 | 167 | 186 | 208 | 206 | 117 |
| DAYS OF RAINFALL | 4 | 2 | 3 | 5 | 11 | 15 | 17 | 17 | 16 | 17 | 14 | 9 |

# Travel Tips

## Tourist Information

### Department of Tourism, overseas offices:

**Australia:** Suite 401, 4/F Thakral House, 301 George St, Sydney, New South Wales 2000, tel: 02 9279 3380, e-mail: info@philippine tourism.com.au web: www. philippinetourism.com.au

**Germany:** Kaiserhofstrasse 7, D-60313 Frankfurt, tel: 069 208 9394, e-mail: info@ diephilippinen.de web: www.wowphilippines.de

**Hong Kong:** Creative Trend, Unit 1109, 11/F New Kowloon Plaza, 38 Tai Kok Tsui Rd, Kowloon, tel: 852 2381 2268, e-mail: info@creativetrend.com www.visitphilippines.com.hk

**UK:** 146 Cromwell Rd, London, SW7 4EF, tel: 020 7835 1100, e-mail: infotourism @wowphilippines.co.uk web: www.wowphilippines.co.uk

**USA:** 447 Sutter St, 5/F, Suite 507, San Francisco, California, 94108, tel: 415 956 4060, e-mail: pdotsf@aol.com web: www.philippinetourism.us www.wowphilippines.us

**USA:** 3660 Wishire Boulevard 900, Suite 216, Los Angeles, California 90010, tel: 213 487 4525, e-mail: pdotla@ aol.com web: see above.

**USA:** 556 Fifth Ave, New York, 10036, tel: 212 575 7915, e-mail: pdotny@aol.com web: see above.

**USA:** 30 North Michigan Ave, Suite 913, Chicago, Illinois, 60602, tel: 312 782 2475, e-mail: pdotchi@aol.com web: see left-hand column.

**Canada:** No office, use nearest US office, e-mail: info@ wowphilippines.ca web: www.wowphilippines.ca

### Local offices:

**Head office:** DOT Building, TM Kalaw St, Ermita, Manila, tel: 02 524 2345, e-mail: webmaster@tourism.gov.ph

**National capital region**, Rm 207, DOT Building, TM Kalaw St, Ermita, Manila 1000, tel: 02 524 2345 or 525 6114, e-mail: ncr@tourism.gov.ph

**Cordillera Administrative Region**, DOT Complex, Governor Pack Rd, Baguio City 2600, CAR, tel: 074 619 1127 or 442 7014, e-mail: dotcar@pldtdsl.net web: www.visitcordillera.com

### Regional Offices:

**I**, Oasis Country Resort, National Highway, Barangay Sevilla, San Fernando, La Union 2500, tel: 072 888 2411, dotregion1@pldtdsl.net

**II**, 29 Rizal St, Tuguegarao, Cagayan 3500, tel: 078 844 5364, e-mail: dotr02 @yahoo.com

**III**, Hilaga Village, San Fernando, Pampanga 2000, tel: 045 477 2499, e-mail: celtour@yahoo.com

**IV**, Rm 208, DOT Building, TM Kalaw St, Ermita, Manila 1000, tel: 02 524 1969 or 542 1528, e-mail: lcjurilla@tourism.gov.ph

**V**, Regional Center Site, Rawis, Legazpi City 4500, tel: 052 481 5593, e-mail: dot_bicol@ yahoo.com

**VI**, Western Visayas Tourism Center, Capitol Ground, Bonifacio Drive, Iloilo City 5000, tel: 033 337 5411, e-mail: deptour6@mozcom.com

**VII**, cor. Legaspi and MJ Cuenco Sts, Cebu City 6000, tel: 032 254 2811, e-mail: dotregion7@gmail.com

**VIII**, Rms 204–5, F Mendoza Commercial Complex, 141 Sto Nino St, Tacloban City, tel: 053 321 2048, e-mail: dotreg8@ yahoo.com

**IX**, Lantaka Hotel By the Sea, Valderrosa St, Zamboanga City 7000, tel: 062 992 6242, e-mail: dotr9@yahoo.com

**X**, A Velez St, Cagayan de Oro City 9000, tel: 088 726 394, e-mail: dotr10@yahoo.com

**XI**, 5/F Landco Corporate Center Building, JP Laurel Ave, Davao City 8000, tel: 082 225 1940, e-mail: dotr11@ yahoo.com

**XII**, 2/F Hua Hing Building, 17 Sinsuat Avenue, Cotabato City 9600, tel: 064 421 1110, e-mail: dotregion12@yahoo.com

**XIII**, G/F Grateful Realty Corp Building, 008 Pili Drive, Butuan City 8600, tel: 085 341 8413, e-mail: dotr13@ yahoo.com

**Web:** www.tourism.gov.ph

www.wowphilippines.com.ph
www.visitmyphilippines.com
www.touristcenter.com.ph
www.itravelphilippines.net

## Entry Requirements

Visitors require a passport valid for at least six months after the intended stay. Travellers from most countries can stay in the Philippines for up to 21 days without a visa if they have a return or onward plane ticket. This can be extended by applying for a 59-day visa (single or multiple entries) which can also be obtained in advance from the Philippine embassies. These visas can be extended in the Philippines by applying to the Commission of Immigration and Deportation. Many travel agencies can handle the paperwork.

## Customs

Passing through Philippine customs is a painless process, with incoming passengers filling in a form before arrival, which is handed to a customs official after immigration. There are no customs formalities when leaving. Those caught with illegal drugs face the death penalty.

## Health Requirements

A yellow fever vaccination certificate is required for travellers from infected areas.

## Getting There

**By Air:** Philippine Airlines (PAL) is the national carrier, serving international destinations in Asia, North America and Australia. Most Asian capital cities and a number of North American cities have direct services to the international airport, Ninoy Aquino, in Manila. Passengers from Hong Kong, Tokyo, Malaysia and Singapore can also fly to Mactan International Airport in Cebu. There are flights from Singapore to Davao. Most European airlines and many Asian airlines fly indirectly to Manila from Europe.

**By Ferry:** The only international ferry links are between Sabah (Malaysia) and the Sulu Islands in the far south.

## What to Pack

The Philippines is a tropical country so visitors staying close to sea level need only light clothing. A pullover is advisable for air-conditioned buildings. Travellers in the mountains will need heavier clothing. In Baguio, temperatures are pleasantly cool even in the day, and at night only a pullover is needed even in January. Those intending to climb mountains will need extensive clothing and their own camping equipment. Surfers should bring their boards and repair kits; facilities are rare. Divers only need their license. Diving is well organized; most dive operators hire out kit. Everyone should bring sunblock, insect repellent and a hat. For photographers, print film is available, though slides and some kinds of digital storage cards are not. Lithium and longlife alkaline batteries can be hard to find outside Manila.

## Money Matters

**Currency:** The Philippine Peso is not a fully convertible international currency, so you are unlikely to be able to buy any before leaving home, or sell any after returning. Inflation fluctuates widely, but at the time of writing (April 2010), is estimated at just over 3%. There are presently about 44.5 PHP (Philippine Pesos) to one US$, 67.9 to the British Pound, and 59.8 to the Euro. The Peso is divided into 100 Centavos, with coins at 1, 5, 25 and 50 Centavos, 1 and 5 Pesos. Notes are 5, 10, 20, 50, 100, 500 and 1000 Pesos.

| CONVERSION CHART | | |
| --- | --- | --- |
| **From** | **To** | **Multiply By** |
| Millimetres | Inches | 0.0394 |
| Metres | Yards | 1.0936 |
| Metres | Feet | 3.281 |
| Kilometres | Miles | 0.6214 |
| Square kilometres | Square miles | 0.386 |
| Hectares | Acres | 2.471 |
| Litres | Pints | 1.760 |
| Kilograms | Pounds | 2.205 |
| Tonnes | Tons | 0.984 |
| To convert Celsius to Fahrenheit: x 9 ÷ 5 + 32 | | |

English • *Pilipino*
Good morning • *Magandang umaga*
Good afternoon • *Magandang hapon*
Good evening •
*Magandang gabi*
How are you? • *Kumusta ka?*
Goodbye •
*Adyos/paalam/sige*
Thank you • *Salamat*
Please • *Paki*
Where can I buy ...? •
*Saan ako makakabili ....?*
How much is it? •
*Magkana ho ito?*
Too expensive! •
*Masyadong mahal!*
Where is....? • *Nasaan ang...?*
When...? • *Kailan...?*
OK • *Sige*
You're welcome • *Walang anuman*
Where is the toilet? • *Nasaan ang kubeta?*
No thanks • *Salamat na lang*
Is there any water? •
*May tubig ba?*
I don't understand •
*Hindi ko maintindihan*
Are we in .... yet? •
*Nasa ... na ba tayo?*
What time will the bus leave?
• *Anong oras aalis itong bus?*
Do you have ...? • *Meron ba kayong ... ?*
I would like some ... •
*Gusto ko ng ...*

**Exchange:** Facilities in Manila are extensive, with banks, hotels, money changers and many shops (especially department stores) changing foreign currency. Rates vary enormously, the best usually offered by money changers. Many Manila banks have ATMs that accept credit and debit cards. Outside Manila and big cities exchange facilities are often limited to the Philippine National Bank. Exchange rates get worse the further you go from Manila. Exchange facilities are limited in Palawan, outside Puerto Princesa. Banks give a poorer exchange rate for travellers' cheques than cash. Banks open 09:00–15:00 Mon–Fri. Money changers are open daily until late evening.
**Credit cards:** Most major credit cards are accepted in cities and major tourist destinations. Credit cards are little used in Palawan.
**Tipping:** This is a widely expected part of life. Airports, ferry ports and bus stations are usually crawling with porters, who survive on what they are given by passengers in return for their help. In taxis it is normal to round up the fare.

## Accommodation

In major cities accommodation varies from simple pensions to five-star hotels. Away from main cities, only cheaper hotels are likely to be available. Air conditioning is available even in many inexpensive hotels. Away from Manila, power cuts and water shortages are common.

## Eating Out

In Manila and Cebu City there is a vast choice, from Filipino dishes, to sushi, Chinese, and American fastfood. Chinese restaurants are widespread, though often serve Filipino interpretations that bear little resemblance to the real thing. Filipino food consists mainly of rice dishes, with meat or fish and very few vegetables. In cities the widest choice of foods can be found at department stores or shopping malls. The best restaurants in small towns are often at the hotels.

## Transport

**Air:** The comprehensive domestic air network links Manila to most places. Flying between two points elsewhere in the country often entails first going to Manila or Cebu and changing planes, though there are plans to improve this. The main carrier is Philippine Airlines (PAL), supplemented on many routes by a plethora of smaller airlines. PAL's domestic routes can be booked from overseas. Web: www. philippineairlines.com www. airphilexpress.com www.zest air.com.ph www.flyseair.com www.cebupacificair.com
**Ferries:** A network of ferries plies among the islands, from large ships, to *bangkas*, outrigger boats fitted with an engine. Long-distance ferries on main intercity routes use large ships, operated by WG&A Lines, Sulpicio Lines and Negros Navigation. The islands of the Visayas used to take a long time to hop among, but a series of high-speed catamaran services have been introduced, linking Cebu, Ormoc, Tagbilaran, Cagayan de Oro, Dumaguete and Dipolog. www.superferry.com.ph www.oceanjet.net
**Trains:** The rail network is very poor. Within Manila the Light Rail Tranist (LRT) line runs north-south. The Metro Rail Transit (MRT) loops around the city. Long-distance trains: the

only passenger line runs to the south of Luzon and links Manila with Legaspi in 10 hours.

**Buses:** Ranging from luxurious air-conditioned to rickety tin cans, thousands of buses ply the roads throughout the country. Comfort may not be guaranteed, but prices are always low. Most services set off in the morning and reach destinations by mid-afternoon.

**Jeepneys:** The uniquely Philippine jeepney serves as the ubiquitous form of local public transport, often taking over where buses leave off. They ply the streets of large towns, provide short-hop services among nearby towns, and connect remote settlements where buses do not go. They can be uncomfortable, crowded and slow, but give a true down-to-earth feel for the Philippines and its people.

**Tricycles and pedicabs:** Both three-wheelers – the former with an engine, the latter relying on pedal power – these are the taxis of most towns. They are inexpensive and convenient, especially if carrying luggage.

**Taxis:** Manila's streets are clogged with taxis, which are now spreading to many other major cities. They are usually air conditioned, and inexpensive. Every taxi is metered, with a fixed flagfall and distance rates. It can be hard to persuade Manila taxi drivers to use the meter if you are carrying luggage or heading to or from the airport. In Cebu City most taxi drivers refuse to use the meter to go anywhere on Mactan Island.

**Car hire:** In Manila, Cebu and some of Luzon's cities (such as Baguio and Subic Bay) self-drive car hire is available. Cars are in reasonable condition and come with full insurance. To hire one, show your country's driving licence (international licences are generally not recognized). You may not take the car on the car ferries linking Luzon and Cebu with other islands. Rates are reasonable and fuel is inexpensive. Driving can be difficult due to congestion and poor signposting.

## Business Hours

Government offices and many private companies: 08:00–17:00 or 09:00–18:00 Mon–Fri. Department stores and many shops: 09:00 or 10:00 to 20:00 or 21:00 daily. Banks: 09:00–15:00 Mon–Fri.

## Time Difference

The Philippines is in one time zone, GMT plus eight hours.

## Communications

Opening times for post offices vary; most open 08:00–17:00. Public telephones can be scarce, except in major cities. In Manila most public phones are card-operated; in many other cities coin-operated (taking one-Peso coins). Most city hotels provide reasonable telephone services, including international calls. Most towns have telephone offices run by the Philippine Long Distance Telephone Company (PLDT) or Bayantel, where calls can be made most times day or night. International phone calls can be expensive. All cell/mobile

phone numbers begin with 09. Internet cafés are common in cities and large towns. They are also frequent in rural areas and at resorts, but connection speeds can be very slow.

## Electricity

Electricity is generally 220 volts, 60 Hz. A few places, such as the old American bases at Subic Bay, Clark and Baguio, have 220 and 110 volt supplies. Round, flat, two- and three-pin plugs are in use.

| NUMBERS | |
|---|---|
| One | isa |
| Two | dalawa |
| Three | tatlo |
| Four | apat |
| Five | lima |
| Six | anim |
| Seven | pito |
| Eight | walo |
| Nine | siyam |
| 10 | sampu |
| 11 | labing isa |
| 12 | labing dal'wa |
| 13 | labing tatlo |
| 14 | labing apat |
| 15 | labing lima |
| 20 | dalawampu |
| 21 | dalawamput isa |
| 30 | tatlumpu |
| 31 | tatlumput isa |
| 40 | apatnapu |
| 50 | limampu |
| 60 | animnapu |
| 70 | pitumpu |
| 80 | walumpu |
| 90 | siyamnapu |
| 100 | isandaan |
| 110 | isandaan sampu |
| 200 | dalawandaan |
| 300 | tatlondaan |
| 1000 | libo |
| One million | angaw |

## PUBLIC HOLIDAYS

**1 January** • New Year's Day
**9 April** • Day of Valour
**Maundy Thursday** • The day
before Good Friday.
**Good Friday**
**1 May** • Labour Day
**12 June** • Independence Day
**30 August** • National Heroes'
Day; a commemoration of
those who gave their lives for
Philippine independence.
**30 November** • Bonifacio Day;
a commemoration of one of the
main leaders of the Philippine
independence movement.
**25 December** • Christmas Day
**30 December** • Rizal Day;
anniversary of the 1896 execution of José Rizal, one of the
first leaders of the Philippine
independence movement.
**31 December** • Special Public
Holiday.

## Weights and Measures

Officially the metric system is
universal, but most Filipinos
are equally at home with
imperial units, happily mixing
pounds, kilos, feet and metres.

## Health Precautions

Although the standard of
hygiene in the Philippines is
reasonable, cholera and other
enteric diseases are present. It
is advisable to be vaccinated
against typhoid and have a
gammaglobulin injection
against hepatitis A. Tap water is
usually safe in Manila, especially at the higher-class hotels,
but one should drink bottled
water, available in country
areas. **Malaria** is present in
many areas below an altitude
of 600m (2000ft). Bring the

appropriate prophylactics.
Another mosquito-borne
disease is **Dengue Fever**.
Increasingly widespread, this
viral disease loves stagnant
fresh water. There is no treat-
ment, except bed rest and fever
control. Avoid it by ensuring
protection from mosquitoes.
Stagnant fresh water may also
be home to **Bilharzia**, so avoid
swimming in such pools, even
if they appear clean. The above
diseases are unlikely. Far more
likely are **dehydration**, **heat
stroke** and **sunburn**. Daytime
temperatures are usually over
30°C (86°F) with humidity at
about 95%, so take care. Con-
sume plenty of liquid and do
not be overactive in the sun;
use sunblock or keep your
body covered or in the shade.

## Personal Safety

The Philippines has had an
image as a rather dangerous
place. However, insurgencies
are mostly a thing of the past.
Theft of property from hotel
rooms, buses and jeepneys can
be a problem. Many hotels
have safety deposit boxes.
Attacks and muggings are rare,
and streets are generally safe.

Women travelling alone are
prone to sexual harassment,
albeit usually fairly mild.

## Emergencies

Emergency numbers vary
around the country. For example, for **police** dial 117 if in
Manila, or 166 in Cebu or
Davao. The emergency num-
ber for **fire** is 757 in Manila,
160 in Cebu, and 110 in
Davao. 911 may also work in
some areas. If using a mobile/
cell phone, regardless of its
country of origin, dialling 112
should automatically link it
through to the local emergency
services.

## Etiquette

Filipinos are easy-going people.
Nevertheless, a few basic
rules are important. Always
be polite and never lose your
temper. Filipinos love to
share, and so if you are
offered something, it may be
bad manners to refuse, even if
you do so with good intentions. Although no one will
ever complain, beach wear is
inappropriate for the town. In
Moslem areas women should
dress conservatively.

## GOOD READING

**Conrad, Joseph** (1899) *Lord Jim,* Penguin.
**Young, Gavin** (1983) *Slow Boats to China,* Penguin.
**Bacho, Peter** (1991) *Cebu,* University of Washington Press.
**Berlow, Alan** (1996) *Dead Season: A Story of Murder and Revenge
on the Philippine Island of Negros,* Pantheon.
**José, F Sionil** (1996) *Sins: A Novel,* Random House.
**Hamilton-Patterson, James** (1998) *America's Boy,* Granta.
**Hicks, Nigel** (1999) *This is the Philippines,* New Holland Publishers.
**Hicks, Nigel** (2000) *The National Parks and Other Wild Places of the
Philippines,* New Holland Publishers.

# INDEX